# Universal Design For Builders

*Building & Selling Accessible, Safe & Comfortable New Homes*

# Universal Design For Builders

*Building & Selling Accessible, Safe & Comfortable New Homes*

## Steve Hoffacker

CAPS, C.E.A.C., MCSP, MIRM

# Universal Design For Builders

## Building & Selling Accessible, Safe & Comfortable New Homes

Cover photo by Steve Hoffacker.

**ALL RIGHTS RESERVED.**

© 2013 by **STEVE HOFFACKER LLC**
West Palm Beach, Florida, USA

ISBN: 978-0-615-84722-1

This book is written for homebuilders (production, semi-production, custom, semi-custom, manufactured, or systems-built) and their new home sales staffs who want to deliver a brand new home — regardless of what type or size it might be, where it is located, or what the general physical needs or family size might be of those who will occupy it — that is comfortable, safe, convenient, and accessible by designing and building with sensible, intuitive universal design and accessibility elements that apply to the widest range of ages and physical abilities.

# Other Aging-In-Place & Universal Design Books By Steve Hoffacker

Other titles for consumers and aging-in-place providers written by Steve Hoffacker are available in print (softbound) and as Kindle eBooks through the author or amazon.com. They include:

"**Common Sense Universal Design:** *Creating Accessible, Safe, Comfortable & Desirable Homes*"

"**Universal Design And Aging:** *Keeping Our Homes Safe, Accessible & Comfortable As We Age In Place*"

"**Universal Design For Safety:** *Creating Safe & Accessible Living Spaces For All Ages*"

"**Power of Discovery For Aging-In-Place Contractors & Providers:** *Who, What, When, Where, & More In Creating A Solution*"

# Table Of Contents

| Chapter | Page |
|---|---|

**Preface** .................................. 11

**1. What Is Universal Design?** ............... 19
    Is Universal Design Real Or A Fad? ......... 19
    Why Is There Universal Design? ........... 20
    What Qualifies As Universal Design? ........ 21
    Why Universal Design Works ............. 23
    Isn't This Just Another Name For "ADA"? ..... 24
    Is Universal Design Considered Green? ...... 24
    Who Benefits From Universal Design? ....... 25

**2. Universal Design As A Solution** .......... 27
    The Universal Design Premise ........... 27
    "Buying Into" Universal Design ........... 28
    The Payoff For Universal Design .......... 29
    The Visitability Benefit ................ 30
    Where Universal Design Works .......... 31

**3. Easy Universal Design Solutions** ......... 33
    What Makes These Solutions Easy? ........ 33
    Lever Door Handles ................. 34

Rocker Light Switches . . . . . . . . . . . . . . . . . 36
Illuminated Light Switches . . . . . . . . . . . . . . 38
Motion Sensor Light Switches . . . . . . . . . . . 39
Photo Cell Light Switches . . . . . . . . . . . . . . 41
Programmable/Preset Light Switches . . . . . . . 42
Digital Thermostats . . . . . . . . . . . . . . . . . . . 43
Door/Drawer Pulls . . . . . . . . . . . . . . . . . . . 44
Single-Lever Faucets . . . . . . . . . . . . . . . . . . 47
Pot Fillers . . . . . . . . . . . . . . . . . . . . . . . . . . 51
Push Button/Keypad Entry Door Locks . . . . . . 53

4. **Important Universal Design Strategies** . . . . . 55

What Makes These Strategies Important? . . . . . 55
36" Doorways . . . . . . . . . . . . . . . . . . . . . . . 56
Open Doorways . . . . . . . . . . . . . . . . . . . . . 59
Wider Hallways . . . . . . . . . . . . . . . . . . . . . 60
Door Swing . . . . . . . . . . . . . . . . . . . . . . . . 62
Closet Doors . . . . . . . . . . . . . . . . . . . . . . . . 63
Trench/Forward/Linear Drains . . . . . . . . . . . 65
Zero-Step/No-Threshold/
 Barrier-Free Showers . . . . . . . . . . . . . . . . 68
Shower Glass/Shower Doors . . . . . . . . . . . . . 69
Wet Room/Shower Room . . . . . . . . . . . . . . . 72
Bath Temperature Setting/Scald Control . . . . . 74
Folding Shower Seats . . . . . . . . . . . . . . . . . . 75
Handheld/Personal Showers . . . . . . . . . . . . . 76
Towel Bars/Hooks/Rings . . . . . . . . . . . . . . . 78
Strategic Grab Bars . . . . . . . . . . . . . . . . . . . 80
Tilt-Out/Tip-Out Sink Front Bins . . . . . . . . . . 82
Body Dryer . . . . . . . . . . . . . . . . . . . . . . . . . 83

# Table Of Contents

    Toe-Kick Lighting . . . . . . . . . . . . . . . . . . . . . 84  
    Under-Cabinet/Task Lighting . . . . . . . . . . . . 85  
    Overhead Lighting . . . . . . . . . . . . . . . . . . . . 86  
    Ceiling Fans . . . . . . . . . . . . . . . . . . . . . . . . . 88  
    Skylights . . . . . . . . . . . . . . . . . . . . . . . . . . . 89  
    Eye-Level Controls . . . . . . . . . . . . . . . . . . . . 90  
    Electrical Outlets . . . . . . . . . . . . . . . . . . . . . 92  
    Wall-Mounted Mirrors . . . . . . . . . . . . . . . . . . 94  

**5. Other Universal Design Strategies . . . . . . . . 97**  
    Additional Strategies For Safety,  
        Convenience, Comfort  
        And Accessibility . . . . . . . . . . . . . . . . . . . 97  
    Contrast And Glare . . . . . . . . . . . . . . . . . . . . 98  
    Flooring . . . . . . . . . . . . . . . . . . . . . . . . . . . 100  
    Automatic Dustpan . . . . . . . . . . . . . . . . . . 105  
    Room-To-Room Transitions . . . . . . . . . . . . . 106  
    Motorized Shelving . . . . . . . . . . . . . . . . . . 107  
    Kitchen Islands . . . . . . . . . . . . . . . . . . . . . 109  
    Modular Sink Base Cabinets . . . . . . . . . . . . . 112  
    Retractable Sink Base Cabinet Doors . . . . . . . 113  
    Cabinets And Drawers . . . . . . . . . . . . . . . . 115  
    Kitchen Desk . . . . . . . . . . . . . . . . . . . . . . . 119  
    Sit-Down Vanity . . . . . . . . . . . . . . . . . . . . . 121  
    Up-Front Controls . . . . . . . . . . . . . . . . . . . 122  
    Easy-Access Appliances . . . . . . . . . . . . . . . 123  
    Wall Blocking . . . . . . . . . . . . . . . . . . . . . . 127  
    Windows . . . . . . . . . . . . . . . . . . . . . . . . . 128  
    Elevators . . . . . . . . . . . . . . . . . . . . . . . . . . 131  
    Chair Lifts . . . . . . . . . . . . . . . . . . . . . . . . . 133  
    First Floor Master . . . . . . . . . . . . . . . . . . . 134

Back-Up Power . . . . . . . . . . . . . . . . . . . . . . 135
Indoor Air Quality . . . . . . . . . . . . . . . . . . . 137

## 6. Universal Design On The Outside . . . . . . . . 139

Why Look At The Exterior? . . . . . . . . . . . . . 139
Zero-Step/Barrier-Free Entrances . . . . . . . . . 140
Lighting . . . . . . . . . . . . . . . . . . . . . . . . . . . 142
Entry Shelves/Tables/Furniture . . . . . . . . . . 142
Covered Entry/Guttering . . . . . . . . . . . . . . 146
Radiant Heating . . . . . . . . . . . . . . . . . . . . 148
Unloading/Landing Area . . . . . . . . . . . . . . 148
Sidewalks . . . . . . . . . . . . . . . . . . . . . . . . . 151

## 7. Universal Design Means Greater Appeal . . . 153

Universal Design Is Differentiating . . . . . . . . 153
Universal Design Is Memorable . . . . . . . . . . 154
Universal Design And Your Sales Process . . . . 155
Utilizing A Team Approach . . . . . . . . . . . . . 157
Now It's Up To You . . . . . . . . . . . . . . . . . . . 158

# Preface

The universal design and accessibility concepts in this text are extracted from my book "Common Sense Universal Design" (available as both a Kindle eBook and paperback edition) and expanded upon just for new home builders, onsite new home salespeople, new home sales managers, new home marketers, architects, and others working with the design, sales, marketing, production, and delivery of new construction to the end consumer — the homeowner.

By contrast, "Common Sense Universal Design" is primarily directed toward remodeling or renovating existing homes and appeals to the homeowner, renter, do-it-yourselfer, remodeler, real estate sales professional, occupational therapist, physical therapist, case manager, interior designer, architect, durable medical equipment supplier, trade contractor, caregiver, consultant, engineer, home inspector, and anyone else interested in creating and achieving accessible, barrier-free living space (inside and out) using the concepts of universal design.

There are many concepts included in that book that the homebuilder can use — and the homebuilder is specifically included in some of the discussion — but I specifically created the book that you are now reading to help you and your team deliver a more desirable product for a larger audience.

As I'll talk about in the following text, there are so many opportunities to swap out, redesign, or re-spec features, fixtures, and devices that normally or historically are included in new homes with something more appropriate, desirable, and functional. Also, there are many ways to create safer, more comfortable, more convenient, more accessible, and more usable living environments — for the original purchaser and for the next owner. This in turn, enhances merchantability, perceived value, value retention or appreciation, and resale value. They also help to make the original sale.

The concepts in this book are based on several years (and counting) of teaching the Certified Aging-in-Place Specialist ("CAPS") designation program through the National Association of Home Builders, the interactions and contributions of the hundreds of attendees at these programs, my independent research, and the remodeling I have done on my own homes.

I have no formal training in architecture or design other than the experience gained in teaching the CAPS program and more than 3 decades of consulting with homebuilders on spatial relationships, consumer preferences, design choices, finishes and styles, sales strategies, and the results of personally conducted market research.

The concepts I discuss in this text have been validated by personal experience in the remodeling of my own homes, focus groups and exit surveys with new home buyers over the years, direct interactions with homebuyers in new home sales centers, and the concurrence and input of hundreds of attendees at my programs.

You'll find as you read what I have prepared for you that universal design is an intuitive approach that works as an effective solution and strategy for many living environments.

In fact, there are few homes anywhere — new construction or existing — that couldn't benefit from the use and application of these principles — unless they were designed that way to begin with or have already been modified.

This is not a concept that is just for the United States or for Canada or even North America. This can be applied to homes anywhere in the world.

The universal design approach accommodates a tremendous range of ages, heights, and physical abilities.

*For specific physical needs that might require more particular design emphasis and solutions, universal design is still an integral part of the overall approach and a great place to begin.*

*New construction is the perfect time to incorporate these universal changes.*

*Whatever these modifications might add to the overall selling price will be offset by the increased perceived value, potential enhanced resale value and market appeal (including more sales), and the proactive inclusion of them so that the homeowners will not need to incur the costs later of having these modifications and renovations done.*

*The more universal design solutions, strategies, concepts, and methods that can be incorporated into the exterior and interior living environment of new construction, the more it will add to the overall safety, comfort, convenience, accessibility, and desirability of the people who are buying your homes — and the people that are invited into those homes or choose to visit your homeowners.*

*Also, the ideas and strategies presented here are based on technology and solutions currently available.*

*It is entirely likely that new products and solutions or even best practices will become available that meet* the definition and spirit of universal design and how it is delivered that also should be considered for use as they become known.

The central theme of this text is creating safer and more desirable living environments by adding universal design elements to make your homes invisibly accessible.

The improvements, solutions, and design strategies we are looking at here — without respect to any particular age group or any specific needs — are those treatments that can be accomplished without looking much different from what they are replacing.

If you were to create specific wheelchair access on the exterior of some of your homes or remove base cabinets under sinks or cooktops when that treatment wasn't needed by a particular homeowner, that might look visibly out-of-place to a casual visitor and call attention to the design.

While some of your new homeowners might want this design incorporated into their new home, we are looking at design solutions that don't suggest how or by whom the space is to be used.

Nevertheless, a wall-mounted or pedestal sink in the powder room or secondary bath or a roll-under countertop or eating area on an island or peninsula would accomplish the same purpose and fit right into any design.

Similarly, grab bars or railings lining the hallway would give an institutional look to many homes — especially when they aren't required for use by everyone.

However, a chair rail (not a dowel or closet rod) that is wide enough in thickness to provide some support or capable of being grasped fits right in.

This book is not intended to address every single area of the home but will provide many solid ideas and strategies on ways to make your designs more accessible, comfortable, attractive, convenient, safe, and desirable.

I also have given you several tips on how to discuss and illustrate the various techniques presented here to your customers so they will understand and appreciate why you have included such designs in your homes or made them available as options.

Whether you are conducting your own presentations as the builder, or your sales team is doing them for you, the same information and strategies apply.

# Universal Design For Builders

*Building & Selling Accessible, Safe & Comfortable New Homes*

# 1

# What Is Universal Design?

### Is Universal Design Real Or A Fad?

Universal design may seem like a fad since it is relatively new and has a large and growing following, but it is real — and it is here to stay.

It makes sense and it offers a very practical solution and strategy for increasing the safety, comfort, convenience, accessibility, and home values for your consumers, regardless of what type of residences you are creating and offering — inside the dwelling as well as around the home and yard on the exterior.

Therefore, it seems to be the real deal.

It's because it offers safe, practical, comfortable, intuitive, unobtrusive, contemporary solutions and styles that I embrace it.

I think you will want to as well — to differentiate yourself from other builders in your marketplace and offer a solid design concept for your homeowners.

This seems to be much too practical to be a passing trend or fad. Its value is borne out in what it provides.

## Why Is There Universal Design?

There may be many good reasons or explanations for universal design to exist and be used in America and elsewhere around the world, but as far as I am concerned, a chief reason for it is the aging of the population.

Of course, none of us likes to think of ourselves as getting older or "aging" so we have to approach it from a different perspective.

The idea of "aging-in-place" or remaining in our homes for as long as we choose and as long as we are able to remain somewhat independent is at the heart of the universal design concept.

Rather than approach the idea of aging in place, however, I prefer the notion of people staying in the homes that they love for as long as they desire.

At some point in life, people will find a home that they like so well that they will want to remain in it.

They are comfortable living in, it generally provides for their needs (or can be adapted to do so), and it's in a neighborhood or location that they like.

This could be a resale or it could be a new home such as you design and deliver.

While someone may already have found their ideal home and is living in it right now, others are still searching for it.

As a homebuilder, you have the perfect opportunity to create new homes for people that have this type of sustainability.

Rather than deliver a home that needs to be modified by the homeowner after delivery to adapt it to the level of comfort, safety, and accessibility they desire, you can provide that for them initially.

## What Qualifies As Universal Design?

Universal design solutions, components, strategies, concepts, and elements are those that appeal to the widest possible audience — regardless of age, physical size, height, weight, or ability.

With the exception of those individuals that require specific design applications for their particular needs and abilities, universal design generally serves quite well for the normal aging process and for those who have various special access needs.

Also, there is no magical age at which universal design becomes attractive. That's the whole idea — that it works for everyone from the very young to the very old.

In 1997, North Carolina State University formulated seven principles of universal design so we now have a measure for determining what is and what is not considered to be within the realm of what we are discussing.

Basically, universal design solutions, fixtures, features, elements, and devices must be accessible and usable by the general population without any advance knowledge or instruction in how to operate something (such as turning on a faucet or light switch or opening a door).

Additionally, they must be so easy and flexible or forgiving to use that it doesn't have to be done perfectly or "just-so" in order to make it work, and must be installed or located in such a way that nearly everyone can reach and use it.

It should require a minimum of effort and not depend on any particular height, hand or arm strength, gripping or grasping ability, or range-of-motion.

When used correctly and appropriately, universal design elements fit seamlessly into the living space and become just part of the home without calling attention to the design or sticking out in anyway as something special or unusual.

Being unobtrusive is a major design objective.

## Why Universal Design Works

In addition to being unobtrusive and just fitting into the normal living environment — whether they are plumbing fixtures, cabinets, countertops, doors, hardware, faucets, switches, controls, appliances, flooring, lighting, or other elements — universal design features enhance the appearance and value of the home.

Putting in such items as a single-lever faucet, a lever door handle, or a rocker light switch (all of which I will talk about in more detail in Chapter 3) makes the home safer for your homeowners, makes controls easier to operate, makes it more convenient for your owners and their visitors or guests, and adds value to the home since people interested in purchasing it at a later date would look for and expect to find such features included.

Resale value is always a concern of homebuyers.

Thus, your home looks more attractive, more inviting for your owners and their guests or visitors, safer, more convenient, more comfortable, and more contemporary (with up-to-date features).

## Isn't This Just Another Name For "ADA"?

"ADA" or the "Americans With Disabilities Act" dictates what must be addressed and in what manner to make indoor spaces and entrances accessible to everyone — especially people using a wheelchair or other forms of mobility assistance.

Universal design solutions, components, strategies, and elements are complementary to that ideal in many ways.

Nevertheless, single family homes, duplexes, triplexes, and quads are exempt from the provisions of ADA although some local building codes could require some compliance.

Designing to comply with ADA requirements may make good sense, and much of what I mention or discuss in this text is consistent with ADA guidelines.

Universal design and ADA are not the same thing, however.

## Is Universal Design Considered Green?

As you read the following text, you will see some suggestions, concepts, strategies, and solutions that seem to be consistent with green building — if you are familiar with green building or consider yourself to be a green builder.

That's true. Green building and universal design have several similarities, but they are not the same thing.

Nevertheless, if you are a green builder, you will see many concepts in this text that you will want to employ in your homes.

They will complement what you already are doing.

Whether you consider yourself to be a green builder or not, the universal design concepts and strategies that I present in this text will help you build safer, more comfortable, more efficient, more convenient, more sustainable, and more accessible homes that have a greater perceived and actual value than similar homes not utilizing these methods.

## Who Benefits From Universal Design?

Essentially everyone can benefit from universal design ideals, strategies, and solutions.

That's why it has the name universal attached to it.

As I mentioned, I already have a book for general consumption on universal design called "*Common Sense*

*Universal Design*." The book you are reading now is similar in many respects, but I want you as a homebuilder to take an active role in using universal design in your product offerings.

Because universal design is meant to accommodate the widest range of ages and abilities, it is not driven by someone's specific physical ability or medical condition. As such, all members of the household can avail themselves of the universal design treatments.

There are many needs-specific solutions that are available, but this text focuses on universal design — products, solutions, strategies, fixtures, devices, and concepts — to appeal to the broadest audience possible and offer a safe, convenient, comfortable, and accessible living environment.

It will give you a larger audience to which you can market your homes and it will save people from needing to make modifications and improvements later because they already are included (or can be made available) in the homes you are offering them.

# 2

# Universal Design As A Solution

## The Universal Design Premise

If we accept the premise that universal design really is for all ages and abilities, it means that it will accommodate the reach, hand and arm strength, range-of-motion, coordination, and physical abilities of a child (say a 4-, 5-, or 6-year old) as well as a 90-year old, and someone who is normally ambulatory to someone who typically uses a walker or wheelchair for assistance.

It follows then that universal design is the preferred design strategy and course of action for creating and modifying living spaces for essentially everyone.

Universal design permits accessibility and use of the various aspects of your home — inside and out— in a safe, friendly, comfortable, and convenient manner without any adaptation or other considerations.

There may be special modifications required to address specific needs in a home, but using the concepts and strategies of universal design will give most people a safer, more comfortable quality of life — regardless of their age or physical ability.

They will hardly notice any of the changes that have been made, and as people age, universal design components will be even more beneficial to them.

Remember as we look at solutions and strategies in this text, that we are talking about things that work for nearly everyone irrespective of their physical age, height, weight, or ability.

Also, it doesn't matter whether they are standing or seated, with full range-of-motion or some limitations, having unrestricted mobility or some mobility issues, with no stamina or coordination issues or moderate ones, and even with some cognitive issues.

In short, universal design offers accessibility, safety, and convenience to all.

## "Buying Into" Universal Design

As a homebuilder, you need to sign on to the benefit of including universal design concepts, ideas, and strategies in your new homes because they make sense, people will appreciate them, you can appeal to a larger audience, and you will increase perceived value (if not the actual selling price) of your homes.

There are six major reasons for wanting and consenting to have universal design strategies and solutions implemented in your homes: safety, comfort, convenience, accessibility, marketability, and visitability.

Any one of these reasons would be sufficient for going ahead with universal design solutions, but most consumers will benefit from all of them.

## The Payoff For Universal Design

Safety is a major objective in any home design, and universal design definitely improves safety.

The reason that universal design elements result in more safety is because they provide more lighting, easier opening drawers and doors, more stable footing and standing surfaces (inside and outside), easier to use controls, less risk of injury or harm, better hygiene, and other helpful solutions for your buyers.

They also provide convenience, comfort, and economic benefits, but mostly they make your living spaces safer.

By making things more accessible and easier to use, generally they are more convenient to use and more enjoyable as well — regardless of how tall someone is, whether they are seated or standing, or what their range-of-motion or other limitations or concerns might be.

Your buyers can be happier, more comfortable, and confident with accessing various fixtures, devices, and appliances in their new home, using water at a pleasant and safe temperature without being concerned about possibly injury, reaching and using controls without having to stretch for them or strain to see what the settings are, and generally moving about in their home.

In terms of marketability, universal design changes and improvements can make your homes more desirable and easier to sell because they will appeal to a broader section of the population and have a higher selling price than similar homes without universal design treatments.

When you create a brand new home this way, you benefit from the increased market appeal, and your customers benefit from the safety, value, convenience, and other factors.

## The Visitability Benefit

A big reason for incorporating universal design changes into your homes is for visitability.

# Universal Design As A Solution

This may be an unfamiliar term for you, but it has to do will the ease or ability — or inability — for anyone to visit someone's home comfortably and conveniently.

Whenever someone entertains or hosts a meeting, party, get-together, or discussion group (and more space for entertaining is a major reason that people shop for a new home), they want people to feel welcome in coming to their home without wondering if they will feel comfortable.

They need this peace-of-mind because they won't always know in advance whether someone can climb steps or negotiate a narrow entryway — when that is the case.

Therefore, creating your new homes to be as "visitable" as possible — capable of being entered and navigated without restrictions or limitations by anyone who wants to visit — will help you both with marketing and sales.

## Where Universal Design Works

To achieve greater safety inside and around your homes, to offer more comfort and convenience (to your buyers and their guests or people who live in your home with you (as well as those who visit overnight), to enhance the value, and to make your new homes easier and more pleasant for anyone to enter and use them, there are many things that can be done — starting with those that are relatively simple and inexpensive that can be done without changing anything you are currently doing except for swapping out what you have been using during the actual installation.

So, we'll start with those easy fixes that involve switches, pulls and knobs, and lighting.

Then we'll move on from there to items that are going to require some modifications to your plans before you begin construction.

No area of the home is going to be exempt from the changes I am suggesting, but the kitchen and bath areas will receive the most attention.

These are, after all, the areas where people tend to spend a lot of their time and the areas that people value the most when shopping for a new home.

As we go along, plumbing fixtures, major appliances, flooring, cabinetry, windows, wall mounted controls, electric outlets, towel bars, mirrors, and similar items will be addressed — along with things such as grab bars, other kitchen and bathroom features, auxiliary lighting, and items for the exterior of the home.

# 3

# Easy Universal Design Solutions

## What Makes These Solutions Easy?

There are several changes that can be made in a new home before it is completed to make it more comfortable, safe, convenient, or accessible that require nothing more than taking out what was planned and replacing it with a more suitable product or item.

Then, as you move forward, these items will be the ones you specify for all of your homes.

These changes make a big, noticeable improvement but require no special effort from what is normally done in building a new home.

The type of modifications and changes this section includes will cover aspects of electrical, plumbing, lighting, doors, and cabinets.

## Lever Door Handles

When I think of universal design, lever door handles are one of the first items that comes to mind.

These are the epitome of universal design.

It truly is a concept that works for all ages and abilities and provides safety, comfort, and convenience throughout the home.

The use of the lever style door handle on all doors that open in or out — including storm doors, screen doors, entrance doors, patio doors, and interior doors, both with and without locks — allow the very young and the very old to use them successfully.

This includes young people who are so short as to be barely able reach the handles with outstretched fingers to those with weakened hand or arm strength or severe range-of-motion limitations who may have difficulty extending their hands or using their fingers to grasp things such as a traditional door knob.

What makes the lever handle such an ideal universal design element is the way it can be operated and the door released to open in several different ways.

It has a large tolerance for error and requires low physical effort.

It can be used with the full hand to grasp it, just a couple of fingers to push down on it, the side of the hand (open or in a fist) to push on it, the back of the hand or wrist to push down, the elbow or forearm to push down, the sides of both hands together to apply enough release pressure when someone's hands are messy or when they are holding something that cannot be put down easily, or even pushing down with a box or something else one might be holding.

This obviously accommodates the full range of ages and many different types of physical abilities, but it has the added practical benefit of being able to be operated when someone's hands are full with something they really don't want to set down or can't put down easily — or when their hands might be messy or greasy and they'd rather not grasp the lever and then have to come back later and clean it.

From a safety standpoint, the levers (unlike traditional knobs and handles) can be operated successfully while wearing a heavy glove or mitten or while using a towel to prevent transfer of whatever someone have on their hands.

From an aesthetic standpoint, the lever handles provide a nice sleek, clean, modern look and are available in several styles, finishes, and colors — with and without locks and for both interior and exterior doors.

A lockset and door handle that is the opposite of universal design and accessibility is the thumb latch style entry lockset that requires sometimes tremendous thumb pressure or pressing down with the side of one's hand to depress the latch enough and then hold it long enough to disengage it from the striker plate and jamb.

This is often a two-handed operation and presents challenges to many people in using it. There is not much tolerance for error in using this.

If you already use the lever door handle on your homes, this is great. Now, you know why they are such a beneficial feature. If not, this is such an easy fix to make.

Whether you already include them or you will be adding them to all of your homes, there is a very real practical application for having them — in addition to just looking nice.

Be sure to point out this feature in your homes and then sell the benefits of this feature during your presentation.

## Rocker Light Switches

I also think of the rocker or "Decora" light switches when I think of universal design. These and the lever door handles top the list.

They each require low physical effort to use them.

Literally anyone who can reach or touch this style of light switch can use it.

Both the door handle and the light switch offer a component of safety, comfort, and convenience in being able to use them so flexibly.

The light switch, like the lever door knob, has tremendous tolerance for error.

Someone can activate it by pushing in the middle or on any other part of it. They can use one finger, the tip of a finger, the flat of their hand, a fist, the side of their hand, the back of their hand, their wrist, their elbow, their shoulder, or even an object that they might be holding in their hand — basically anything that provides enough contact and pressure to move the switch into the on or off position.

Again, if someone is holding something or their hands are dirty and they don't want to make a mark on the switch, switchplate, or wall, the rocker or Decora switch is great.

Contrast this with the tiny toggle-style switch that typically must be grasped or pushed with more physical effort and with greater accuracy that the rocker switches — there is no comparison.

In terms of aesthetics, the rocker or Decora switches provide a clean, modern, contemporary look, while the toggle switches look a little old-fashioned.

The rocker switches are a great universal design solution, but in many ways they are just the accepted style to use.

They definitely fit in and are probably more noticeable when they aren't used than when they are.

You might already be using this style of switch because of its appearance.

Nevertheless, there is a very practical reason for using them as well.

Again, accent these design benefits during your sales presentation with your customers, and use the phrase "universal design" if it resonates with your customers.

## Illuminated Light Switches

As long as we are talking light switches, they can be obtained in the rocker or Decora style with a small light in them that makes them easy to find in dim light or at night.

Simply take out the existing switches and replace them with these.

This is an easy change that can translate into a big benefit during your sales presentation.

This adds safety and convenience (and a memory or discussion point) — plus the comfort of knowing that the light switch can be located.

## Motion Sensor Light Switches

In swapping out light switches from toggle to rocker or Decora — or even if you already use the rocker or Decora switches — a motion sensor (also called motion detector) light switch that mounts in the same space as the switch it is replacing can provide peace-of-mind and added safety as well as convenience in low traffic areas.

The switch turns on any light that is controlled by it — ceiling fixture or lamp with incandescent, florescent, LED, or halogen bulbs — and stays on for either a fixed period of time or for a time that can be set to turn off the lights after the sensor detects no movement in the room.

Anyone who enters a darkened room — such as a powder room or guest bedroom — with something in their hands to put away in that room (paper goods, towels, linens, or clean laundry) or just unfamiliar with the room can take care of their mission without being concerned about locating or using the light switch. This works great for visitors and guests also.

This also provides a measure of security by having lights that come on as if someone in the home has turned them on — when someone or something not expected to be present is detected.

A similar idea with less flexibility than having a light come on when someone enter a room and turn off when they leave is to use an electric timer that plugs into an electrical outlet.

It allows one or more lamps to plug into it and be turned on and off at fixed times that you determine and set.

This works well for holiday or decorative lighting in your model homes and sales center as well as allowing you to leave various lights on for security and aesthetics.

For exterior lighting, fixtures are available that are solar powered so they literally can be placed anywhere — on the fascia, on a pole, on a fence, on a porch railing or post, on the garage — without needing electric wiring to run them.

They are operated by a motion sensor and powered by solar energy. The solar collectors just need the ability to be recharged during the day by being mounted where they will receive sunlight.

You provide additional lighting for your customers with no additional energy expense.

## Photo Cell Light Switches

This is another alternative for exterior lighting and indoor lamps that only need to be on at night. This strategy adds safety, comfort, and convenience to the living space.

A photo cell that is part of the light fixture or a separate sensor switch that is screwed into the light socket with the bulb then screwed into it will turn the lights on that it controls when the ambient lighting has dropped to a low enough level to require the lights to come on.

They will stay on until sufficient daylight causes them to turn off. However, they sometimes will come on and remain on when the sky is very cloudy or during a heavy rain or snowfall.

The important thing to remember is to aim the photo cell sensors away from other lights that might interfere with their sensory ability and to generally have exterior sensors facing north or east.

While this may not be something that you would necessarily include in your homes, it would be great to use in your models and sales center.

I typically recommend that all lights in a model be turned on during business hours to give the greatest amount of light possible, to illustrate where the light fixtures are located, and to show your customers that all of them work.

However, with the sensor switches, you may want to attach a few of your indoor lights to them to illustrate to your customers that you use and recommend them (even if you don't include them in your home package) and that you are conserving energy during daytime hours by not using lights that don't need to be on.

During normal bright sunlight, you or your sales team can cover a sensor to show how the light comes on and that it does work.

**Programmable/Preset Light Switches**

This is another safety, convenience, and efficiency option available.

Whether the lights come on with a sensor or are turned on manually, a device that still fits into a standard switch box can use preset times — that come with the switch for the light or lights controlled by the switch — to remain on for a fixed period of time (for instance, 5 or 10 minutes).

It also can be programmed by you or your homeowners to stay on for a certain period of time before turning off the lights.

For any of these devices that I have mentioned for controlling when the lights come on or turn off, there are several manufacturers, brands, models, styles, sources, and price points available.

## Digital Thermostats

This solution is similar to the light switch improvements for additional convenience and comfort, and this allows anyone in the home to access and use the device.

That's what makes it universal.

It's just a matter of taking out or changing over from an older type manual, dial-type or slide-switch style mercury thermostat and replacing it with one that has a digital display — programmable or not.

Some thermostats have the ability to set and control temperatures for various times of the day or for multiple days. Some just maintain the temperature as it is set — for heating or cooling.

Either way, they can be read from a few feet away and don't rely on grasping a dial or switch and trying to move it a small amount. Some can even be controlled remotely from smartphones and tablets.

Obviously, this is good for all ages and even people with some vision difficulties.

It is certainly much easier to read the display with a specific temperature number than trying to determine the settings and temperature on a non-digital one since the numbers are larger and are usually lit on the digital type — it's also easier to set the precise desired temperature.

This change-out can be made exactly where is has been planned or traditionally located, but an even better strategy is to locate it no higher than 48" above the floor so it is more accessible to everyone.

This will require moving the wiring a little during construction to accommodate the lower, more convenient, more accessible position.

You might already be including the digital thermostat in your homes, but lowering it is a strategic design change.

### Door/Drawer Pulls

People with small hands, weak hand or arm strength, or arthritis in their hands or fingers may have trouble grasping small door and drawer pulls or handles to use them effectively.

Installing better pulls and knobs is a logical change to your design that will make it easier for everyone to use them to access the cabinetry.

# Easy Universal Design Solutions

This one change can make a huge difference.

In addition to making it easier, more comfortable, and safer for everyone to use, this change can really dress up the appearance of a kitchen or bath.

We want to achieve door and drawer handles and pulls that require little-to-no physical effort or gripping to operate — unlike that needed for using small knobs.

You might already have made this change just from market demand or your own design preferences. If not, this is an easy change to make before the cabinets are ever delivered and installed.

The more space between the drawer or door pull and the drawer or door surface, the better it is so that more of someone's hand can engage the pull. Also, there is more tolerance for using it effectively this way.

The major safety concern for selecting new pulls is that any material on the pull surface that sticks out pasts the mounting posts on the main part of the pull can catch clothing or skin when someone walks by too closely or comes in contact with it.

By eliminating this extra material, you can accent this feature during your sales presentation and stress how you have your customer's safety and comfort in mind.

An alternate to using door pulls is to use a magnetic latch that holds a door closed and then releases it by depressing the lock slightly with the door front to "pop" it open.

Some doors also will remain closed with tension or spring assisted hinges or just the weight of the door without a catch — and open by grasping a corner or edge of the door and gently pulling on it. Such doors typically do not have a door pull and provides a cleaner, more uniform look that way.

The issue with doors that have no pulls on them — or ones that don't use the pulls to unlatch and open the doors — is that they aren't as intuitive to use and may be confusing for guests or visitors.

For instance, does one push on the door or attempt to grasp an edge and pull it open? Where should someone push — along the top edge or the side, in the middle or toward one corner?

If it's not a magnetic spring release latch, what if someone can't open it with just their fingertips?

These issues with the doors and drawers that do not have visible pulls may not be enough of a concern to eliminate their use and switch to installing pulls, but being intuitive and easy to use are key objectives of universal design.

## Single-Lever Faucets

When I think of universal design, another one of the first items that comes to mind is the single-lever faucet — for safety, comfortable application, accessibility, and convenience.

Again, this is a classic example of universal design. It truly works for all ages and abilities, and it's already included in many homes just because it looks nice.

The single-lever faucet is more stylish and contemporary than two-handle faucets, although fancy and rather expensive two-handle faucet sets can be purchased.

That really isn't the point — how fancy or expensive they are.

Aside from offering a sleek, modern look, the single-lever faucet offers significant safety, convenience, and accessibility benefits over the two-handle style.

While you might typically install the two-handle faucets in the kitchen, bath, laundry, garage, basement, or other wet areas in the home, the single-lever faucet is a much more practical and safe fixture. Consider discontinuing the use or availability of two-handle faucets — especially in the kitchen, and not even offering them as an option — for these reasons.

A single-lever faucet can be operated by anyone who can reach it without being overly concerned about someone accidently burning or hurting themselves by getting hot water unexpectedly.

The faucet handle and mixer would have to be positioned to the far left and have the hot water come on rather instantly for this to be a concern.

Contrast that with someone using a sink with two faucet handles and not paying attention, realizing, or understanding that the left side is the hot water control and being indifferent to the water temperature as long as they were able to have water coming out — until it may be too late to avoid discomfort or a mild burn.

Another safety benefit that the single-lever faucet affords, that likely everyone can appreciate and relate to, is being able to use it while we are preparing food.

After handling raw meat or fish or having sauces or something sticky or messy on our hands, we can turn on the faucet and have the water come on without needing to touch the handle with our hands. There are several other ways of activating the lever without grabbing it.

The same is true when anyone is doing other work around the house or yard that might leave their hands dirty, oily, muddy, or greasy.

Depending on the type and size of the lever you select and install (or make available) in your homes, the faucet can be turned on with the forearm, fist, wrist, back of the hand, elbow, while wearing kitchen gloves or using a towel and using it to grip the faucet handle to avoid direct contact, a wooden spoon or other kitchen utensil, or even a bowl or pot that someone might be holding.

There are many ways to activate the faucet without actually grasping the handle because the concept is so flexible — a hallmark of universal design.

There also are faucets available now that have sensors or just require some type of light contact along the spout to activate the water flow — less intuitive but very convenient.

Generally, the water temperature is more consistent with a single-lever faucet than the two-handle system when the water is turned off and then back on again because the temperature mixing does not have to be redone.

Although the water temperature is subject to cooling off depending on the length of time that has passed since turning off the single-lever faucet, the water is relatively the same temperature as it was when it was turned off (or it soon will be as soon as it heats back up) — without adjusting the faucet handle position.

With a two-handle faucet system, the water has to be remixed by turning on each handle and then testing the water temperature until it feels about the way it was previously — unless it had been turned on with only cold or only hot water.

This is another safety and convenience benefit of using the single-lever faucet — throughout the home.

Another universal design gadget that is available — for those spouts that will accept them — is a screw-on adapter in the place of a typical aerator that provides a blue light or red light to the water stream to indicate its relative temperature.

This is an immediate visual clue for the general water temperature as well as great fun for kids and a conversation starter and attention getter during your sales presentations — as long as no one is startled by it.

Another option is selecting a faucet that already has a built-in light to indicate the relative temperature.

One additional safety, comfort, and convenience issue to remember involves the choice of the faucet spout to provide enough room to get your hands under the flowing water and also to reduce splashing and spray.

Therefore, make sure the water is delivered a comfortable distance away from the back of the sink.

Some faucets have very short spouts and it is hard to get your hands or a dish or pot totally under the water without contacting the back of the sink.

Another consideration is excess spray or splash from a spout that is too high (resulting in a lot of splash or water bounce off the bottom of the sink to the surrounding countertop, floor, or person using the sink) or angled to the point that water tends to hit the bottom of the sink and refract directly out onto the person using it.

Both cases present safety, comfort, and convenience issues.

Shallow bowls and vessel sinks (because of their shape) tend to create more splash issues than others.

## **Pot-Fillers**

A type of single lever faucet that is often used or requested in the kitchen is the pot filler.

I caution against using this. It is not a universal design strategy and can create unforeseen and unpleasant issues for the homeowner.

It typically is located in the backsplash above the stove or cooktop — although I have seen them on an island or at the sink.

The issue is one of safety. It certainly supplies convenience — being able to fill a stockpot, saucepan, or double boiler right from the cooking surface.

What happens that makes it unsafe and not a universal design strategy is that it gives people a false sense of well-being.

They are struck by the convenience of filling their cooking vessel right at the stove or cooktop and don't relate the weight of the water to what they are doing.

Since they are not filling the pot or pan at the sink and then walking with it over to the stove or cooktop, they have no idea how much it might weigh or if they can pick it up or move it after they are done using it — even if only some of the liquid remains.

After the cooking is complete, they may find that they cannot lift the pot from the stove or cooktop — because of the volume and weight of the water or the height of the cooking surface, or both.

They risk spilling or splashing it on themselves or the floor and may find that they have to bail the liquid into smaller containers before being able to lift the pot.

Range of motion issues, physical height, and physical strength eliminate many people from being able to use this.

Youngsters who want to help out in the kitchen could not access the pot filler or move the heavy pot.

The same goes for seniors or grandparents who might be fixing dinner.

This fixture is modern and attractive, but because of the safety and accessibility issues concerned with using it, it likely will never be used by a homeowner more than a couple of times — if at all.

You can easily sell the benefits of not including it and even position yourself strategically against your competition that does offer it.

I wouldn't suggest offering it as an option either for the reasons mentioned here.

## **Push Button/Keypad Entry Door Locks**

This is an easy replacement for existing entry door locksets. Make sure to get one with a lever handle.

Simply swap out the one that that you have been using and replace it with the keypad lockset.

This works for all ages.

Young children who can be trusted with the combination can let themselves into the home. There is no worry of them losing a key or trying to keep track of how many people have been issued keys.

Everyone in the household can unlock the door by just punching in the correct combination, and the lock can be reprogrammed as often as desired for additional security.

Remembering a combination could be an issue with people who have short term memory loss, but then using a key is likely an issue as well.

An additional safety, convenience, and safety benefit of the keypad lock is that it can be programmed with a separate combination for temporary access each time repair and service technicians or personnel need to enter the home — so that the actual combination is not handed out or revealed, and there is no need to have a key given to them or hidden for them.

Locks also are available with fingerprint readers to unlock and open them.

These are all good selling benefits as well.

# 4

# Important Universal Design Strategies

## What Makes These Strategies Important?

In addition to the several changes we just looked at that require hardly any work, planning, or redesign other than swapping, changing, or re-spec'ing less efficient or effective light switches, door handles, cabinet and drawer handles, door pulls, and faucets, there are several changes that can be made in a new home — as it is being designed or completed — to make it more comfortable, safe, convenient, or accessible (and even valuable) that require some advance planning and thought.

These changes will make a big, noticeable impact on the general safety and comfort of the living space you are creating.

However, in keeping with the objective of universal design to keep things as invisible as possible, these changes won't necessarily be obvious to those not familiar with the way the home would have looked previously.

That's why these changes are very strategic and great selling features.

Your competition will likely not be offering these even though they should.

## 36" Doorways

This is another one of the items that tops my list when I think of universal design.

It is such an intuitive solution, but it has yet to be embraced by the majority of the nation's homebuilders.

Thus, you have an opportunity to really distinguish you and your company in this regard and to position yourself positively in your marketplace.

If more homes came with 36" doorways already included, homeowners would not have to incur the time, expense, and inconvenience (regardless of who does the work) of replacing the existing doors with larger ones later on as they discover that they aren't large enough for general access.

# Important Universal Design Strategies

Unless 36" (or "3-0") interior doorways are specifically requested by new home purchasers in semi-custom or custom homes, most of the new homes being built are designed and built with 32" ("2-8") or smaller interior doorways.

The difference in wall space between a 32" and 36" doorway is 4", but that is a very important 4" for universal design and accessibility — and for the general comfort and convenience of your future homeowners.

Your customers will immediately notice the wider doorways and will comment on it — if you don't point it out first. This is a huge selling feature.

The practical reason for all interior doorways being 36" wide — many exterior doorways already are 36" (or larger when double doors are used) — is for ease of moving furniture about in the home.

Anyone who has ever moved a mattress or bed frame into a bedroom — or other furniture from room-to-room in a home or apartment — knows how challenging it can be dealing with a 32" or smaller doorway compared to one that is 36".

Skinned knuckles, bruised shins, and dinged furniture — or even getting furniture stuck or wedged into the doorway opening — have resulted from narrow doorway openings.

It's sometimes hard enough to fit through or deal with a 36" doorway, but that is so much better than contending with smaller, narrower ones.

Just for giving everyone an easier time of moving furniture or other items between rooms in the home is reason enough to have the wider doorways.

The visitability factor comes into play when we note that a wheelchair may need 29" or more of clearance to negotiate safely through a doorway.

While a 32" doorway is wide enough in theory for wheelchair access, it doesn't measure up. When you allow for a door thickness of 1⅜" or more, a hinge that accounts for another ¾" or so, and the stop (nearly another ⅝"), the effective clearance in a 32" doorway has been reduced by some 2¾" or more.

In order to achieve a true 32" or larger effective passageway for easy wheelchair access in a home, 36" doors are the minimum size that should be used.

Currently, they are the widest size of a pre-hung hinged door commonly available.

In some cases, pocket doors — mounted inside the walls — or sliding doors (also called "barn doors") — hung along the inside or outside walls of the doorway — may provide a wider effective opening as well.

Mounting inside the walls may require some moving of planned electric wiring and light switches.

Surface mounted doors do not require any major construction — just installing the track and hanging the door along with finishing the casing and door jamb in the doorway opening to leave an attractive appearance.

Using a sliding hanging door or a pocket door will create some talking and memory points in addition to being functional.

To swap out the 32" or smaller door with the 36" door, you may have to modify your framing plans and relocate your electrical service runs.

Wider hallways may be necessary as well, and the space will need to be taken from the rooms bordering the hallway — or a slightly larger floor plan will be required.

## Open Doorways

A great universal design solution that is aesthetic as well as practical is creating the illusion of a doorway for dividing space or separating rooms without actually installing an operating door.

This design technique is used frequently as an architectural element, but you can use it as part of your overall universal design strategy for both style and function.

These open doorways — cased openings — can be nearly as wide as the hallway or space they are framing.

On long entry halls that take people from the front of the home to the back, such a feature (sometime with a glass transom over it) can be used to define the separation of the front of the house from the back, but no door needs to be mounted because there is no need to close off the space.

Archway passages as entrances to a master suite vestibule or a secondary bedroom wing function the same way. They act as a doorway but remain open at all times because there is no door attached to them.

They can also be used the same way as entrances for dining rooms or family rooms to indicate where the spaces begin but being totally accessible.

These open passageways allow wide, unrestricted access and passage by anyone in the home and facilitate movement of furniture as well.

## Wider Hallways

This idea goes along with 36" doorways but takes a lot more planning and work to accomplish.

# Important Universal Design Strategies 61

This is not a matter of just removing a door and making the opening larger. We are talking about moving walls — at least one and likely two or more.

A typical interior hallway in a home is 36" or less, and that obviously can't accommodate a 36" doorway at the end of the hallway or comfortable passage along the hallway by anyone in a wheelchair or walker.

To make hallways wider, the rooms with a common wall with the hallway will necessarily become smaller unless more space is added to the entire floor plan or taken from another area of the home.

If rooms away from the hallway are modified to create more space for the rooms adjacent to the hallway, care must be exercised so that the resulting sizes are still functional and competitive.

Residual factors to consider — but worth it for what you achieve in terms of accessibility and visitability — include possibly relocating, repositioning, or adjusting the locations and length of runs for wiring, plumbing, and air conditioning or heating ductwork.

Hallways that are 42-45" in width seem to be field-tested and reasonable.

Adding wall blocking inside the hallway walls is a great example of adaptable design and a great selling benefit when the homeowner (or a subsequent owner) at a future date might need or desire it for installing grab bars or railings for a specific need in the household. This could be an optional element just for those buyers who want it.

## Door Swing

Occasionally, interior or exterior doors open from the wrong side or in the wrong direction for the convenience, safety, and accessibility of those in the household — or those shopping for the new home.

The hinges need to be switched left-for-right or right-for-left — due to the amount of room near the latch or door handle side of the door and the room to approach it and open it easily.

It could also be a matter of what the door opens into or onto in terms of an adjacent wall, cabinets, fixtures, or furniture, built-ins, or furnishings.

You may not have studied this previously or you may have relied on your architect or CAD program to select what appeared to be effective space utilization.

However, the way that interior doors open in terms of direction — left or right, or in or out — can make a huge difference to the occupants and even whether a home is considered desirable enough to purchase.

Sometimes it's the little things like this that might cause a potential buyer to pass when they really like other aspects of the floor plan.

Of course, you can offer reversing the door swing from side to side, so that it opens opposite of where it is now but still in or out the same, as an option, but a better, more universal design way of approaching it would be to determine the safest, most convenient, and accessible way for the door to open and then install it that way.

Make sure to point out to your customers during your sales presentation why you did this and how most builders do not pay attention to such details.

The same goes for reversing whether the door opens in or out (except where local building codes require certain doors to open a particular way).

## **Closet Doors**

There are many different styles of closet doors, depending on what room the closet is located in and what the purpose of the closet is.

There are bedroom closets — both wall closets with bypass, sliding, hinged, pocket or bi-fold doors as well as walk-in closets with pocket, sliding, bi-fold, or hinged doors.

There are linen, coat, and utility closets in the hallway or foyer as well as linen and supply closets in the bath.

There is the pantry and possibly laundry closet space in the kitchen (sometimes the hallway) for the washer and dryer.

The same comments about door swing apply to closets in terms of accessibility and ease of use.

An additional consideration is that the door must remain open while the closet is in use rather than just being opened to pass through it or closed for privacy like other doors in the home.

Therefore, you need to take a hard look at how each door is used before deciding if they need to be redesigned or allowed to remain as they have been planned.

Evaluate the approach space to make sure that it is safe and adequate.

Look at the way the door is opened and the impact it has on adjacent space or furniture while it remains in the open position, see if there are any potential obstructions preventing the door from opening fully or allowing others in the home to walk past it while it is open, and assess how easy it is to open and close the door to gain access to the closet.

# Important Universal Design Strategies

For in-line pantry and linen closets that are part of the cabinetry, dividing the space into smaller compartments with smaller doors is better so that the doors aren't so heavy and that just one area of the closet or pantry can be accessed as needed rather than opening a large door to the entire space.

Again, these are selling features for convenience, safety, comfort, and accessibility.

## Trench/Forward/Linear Drains

In a traditional bathtub — with or without a fixed shower head installation or handheld shower — the drain is located forward.

It is at the end of the tub — typically under the fill spout and the faucet handles or mixer and at the end opposite of where someone typically steps into the tub.

However, in a stall shower — either manufactured or constructed on site — the drain in the shower pan is located in or near the middle. The floor of the shower is formed into an inverse pyramid with the drain at the center.

Even when the floor of the shower is formed without using a manufactured pan, it is still constructed with the same design and shape.

I think the drain on a standard bathtub is in the correct spot for beneficial safety and comfort reasons and that most showers have it wrong.

First, the function of a shower is to get clean by washing away dirt with soap and water.

Do we really want to stand in used soapy water while it drains — sometimes slowly and hindered because we are standing on the drain? Our feet and ankles never get totally clean until we move away from the drain and rinse them again after most of the water completely drains.

Second, we have uneven footing because of the way the floor slopes and pitches to the drain — from four different planes. This can be a slipping and balance issue.

Many times, we find ourselves standing right on the drain — which is not particularly comfortable and hinders the function of the drain.

For anyone needing to use a transfer bench or shower chair, it is very hard to position it easily and keep it in one place.

Third, we often have to move about to try to get away from the water that is pooling at the drain, and this can result in slippery footing and potentially a fall.

Finally, if we want to stand on something such as a shower mat, a teak platform, or nonslip treads, these do not conform well to the inverse pyramid design and must be adapted for use and to keep them from covering or blocking the drain.

The solution to this safety and comfort issue is to move the shower drain back to the front of the shower like it is in the tub.

The faucet, mixer, and shower head may be fine where they are. The drain is the main issue.

To allow water to drain faster and provide a sleeker look to the shower, a trench or linear drain is recommended.

The plumbing below the drain remains the same with just the way the water is collected on the surface changing.

There are even surface drains that look much like the flush deco-drains used on pool decks that come in a variety of finishes, colors, and patterns.

Using a trench or linear drain that is located at the end of the shower ("forward") like it is in a traditional tub, with a flat shower floor gently pitched toward the drain, offers efficient draining and greater footing stability, accommodates the use of chairs or benches in the showers, and allows application of nonslip floor treatments.

Also, if someone else needs to be in the shower to offer assistance to a child or adult, it is easier for them to stand and move about on a flat service and one without the water pooling in the center.

It may take a little redesign, but this change should be relatively easily to accomplish and will be a huge selling feature. If you want to allow your customers a choice of drain styles and colors, you can do that as an option you aren't currently offering.

### Zero-Step/No-Threshold/Barrier-Free Showers

When there is just a shower present with no bathtub, changing out the lip, curb, threshold, transition, or step-up at the shower entrance to allow level access between the bathroom floor and the shower floor eliminates possible slipping, range-of-motion, balance, and coordination issues as one steps from one surface to another — entering or leaving the shower — and allows free access to the shower by anyone.

It may look a little different than traditional showers that have a lip, step up, curb, or raised shower pan, but this "zero-step" shower entrance is becoming more popular and eliminates many of the safety and access concerns normally present.

Again, your reasons for doing this — to accommodate a wider range of the population and allow basically anyone to access the shower without hindrance — should play well with your customers.

## Shower Glass/Shower Doors

To keep as much water inside the tub or shower as possible while taking a shower or using the handheld shower, some bathtubs and showers have shower doors installed.

Generally, a single hinged door is used for a walk-in or stall shower, and a two- or three-panel bypass set of doors is used for a tub.

The tub doors are mounted in a track that covers the bath opening and slide inside and along a top and bottom track to keep water from splashing outside the tub or shower and onto the bathroom floor.

The lower track is held in place with adhesive caulk and the weight of the two or three doors. The side tracks are fastened to the walls or sides of the bath/shower area with screws or wall fasteners. The top track simply rests in place atop the two sides and has the weight of the doors keeping it in place.

Just adding the extra height and width of the lower track is enough to create a potential tripping hazard or entrance barrier for those people with balance or coordination issues, those with relatively short legs, and those with range-of-motion issues in the hips, ankles, or knees.

One-piece shower doors for stall showers may open into the shower or out into the room and generally have magnetic or ball closures that open rather easily and allow most anyone to use them.

However, they can easily release and pop open when fallen against or used for support during a slip — increasing the likelihood of a more serious fall and injury.

If they have a locking mechanism strong enough to prevent opening with incidental or light contact, they can create a safety hazard of a different nature and not be suitable for use by those not strong enough to operate the door.

They also can impact the area of approach and clearance around the shower (as well as inside it from a safety standpoint) as sufficient space needs to be allowed for people to open the door freely — and for the doors to be opened or left in the open position and not obstruct access to anything else in the bathroom.

Outside of the issue of maintaining the glass or plexiglas panels to keep soap scum and mildew from forming or building up on the surface, there are other safety concerns and issues with the bypass doors and even the clear glass panels that are often used as walls or dividers along with shower doors to define the wet space and prevent water from getting into the rest of the room when the shower is used.

The soap or other build-up on the surface can make the surfaces slippery when touched or leaned against — from incidental contact to being used to try to keep from falling after a slip or loss of balance.

Depending on how they are installed and the type of glass used, the panels may not be able to support someone's weight or withstand a fall into it in a panic situation such as loss of balance, a slip, or fall.

If these glass panels were to break, flex, or dislodge from their mounts or supports, a more serious accident than just a fall could result.

Additionally, the glass doors and glass panels can reflect and refract light in a way that creates glare and affects orientation, depth perception, or the ability to tell where objects are.

Many of them also have towel bars attached which — in a panic situation — are used as grab bars and may break, pull loose, or cause the doors to come out of their tracks or otherwise fail to offer the support required.

In general, there are so many reasons of a safety, convenience, comfort, and accessibility nature for not using glass around a shower or bath area and not that many good ones that support their use.

Suggest not including them in your homes. Don't offer them as an option either — for all of these reasons plus general maintenance and warranty.

## Wet Room/Shower Room

A solution for any size secondary bathroom — and particularly a smaller one where creating a zero-step shower entrance presents additional challenges for keeping the rest of the room from getting wet when the shower is used — is to make the entire bathroom a wet room or shower room.

When the bathroom cannot be designed larger due to a price point or the size required for the other rooms in the home, a wet room is a good idea.

This further eliminates the need to consider adding glass partitions, shower doors, and shower curtains.

It also allows the shower to be as large as necessary in the room without specifically defined boundaries. Whether one or more fixed shower heads or a handheld/personal shower are used, the water from the shower doesn't have to stay in a confined space.

# Important Universal Design Strategies

This accommodates a wide range of ages and abilities.

Because all of the walls and floor (and often the ceiling) are tiled, any water from the shower will drain to the central floor drain.

This drain can be located under the shower head, or it can be installed linearly (as a deco-drain) from wall-to-wall (and parallel to the entrance door) along the general edge of the shower area.

The floor would need to be pitched correctly for proper drainage.

Essentially, with this concept the bath is designed in such a way that most anything in it can get or be wet — just make sure to locate the toilet paper holder, towel bars, and cabinetry away from direct water contact or spray as much as possible.

Pedestal sinks or wall mounted sinks may do well in such an application to save space and make the use of cabinetry unnecessary.

Tankless and corner toilets can save some space also and create memory points for your customers.

Pocket doors or sliding doors may maximize the interior space without adding a door physically opening into the space — or out into the hallway.

This concept should be easy to sell to your customers.

Anyone, from youngsters to people who need assistance bathing, can use such a space comfortably and maintenance is easy since all of the walls are tiled.

There is nothing that says the entire room has to get wet when the shower is used, but this design doesn't require water just to remain in a small space.

## Bath Temperature Setting/Scald Control

One way to avoid accidentally using water that is uncomfortably or dangerously hot in the bath or shower — and risking possible injury — is by setting the hot water heater to a maximum temperature of 120°.

Most dishwashers and washing machines have the heating ability within them to create the temperature above this that they need to perform properly. So, a lower hot water temperature may be the solution.

Still, many people may prefer a hotter temperature for a shower or for washing dishes by hand.

The safety and comfort solution here — and one regardless of ability or needs — is a temperature or scald control for the tub or shower. It can be set for the desired temperature to keep the water from getting any hotter than what is selected.

Again, this will be a memory point and an attention getter.

## Folding Shower Seats

Some people need to sit down or rest routinely in order to use the shower and bathe comfortably and effectively.

If this is the case, they should have a seat installed or integrated into the shower design.

This is easily done during new construction and can be a great selling feature — even if not everyone in the household requires it.

However, as a component of universal design, a folding seat is a good strategy that offers safety, comfort, and convenience for everyone.

A seat that is out of the way except when needed serves everyone.

People who required it all the time can leave it fully deployed, or you can build one in.

For people who require it occasionally, the folding seat can be opened into the operational position, used, and then stored again against the wall when they are finished.

Overnight or longer-term house guests can take advantage of it as well.

It can be designed in a variety of sizes and materials — as long as they are suitable for a wet area and can be cleaned easily.

Whether it's sitting to let the water massage a muscle pull or general muscles aches, sitting to keep stitches or surgical sites in the lower leg or foot from getting wet, sitting because of fatigue, sitting to shave one's legs, or bathing small children or others who require assistance, a fold-down seat accommodates a wide range of users.

It can be used when necessary and then stored away when it isn't needed.

A kitchen and bath designer or a durable medical equipment specialist may be a good consultant for this project.

Again, this will be a memory point and something people will be talking about positively.

### Handheld/Personal Showers

The handheld or personal shower is a great universal design strategy that offers safety, comfort, and convenience to all.

It can be an auxiliary shower to an existing fixed showerhead or the only showering device in a bathtub or stall shower.

It may be mounted along a slide bar, rest on a holder, or it might retract into the tub fixture.

When the handheld or personal shower is mounted along a slide bar where the height of it can be adjusted up or down along the length of the bar, you'll find that some people will choose to leave it in place and just use it as a wall-mounted shower.

Others will remove the shower head from the mount and hold it.

When a folding or stationary shower seat is used, the handheld shower — with sufficient hose length — can easily be used by someone while they remain seated.

For bathing children or when other bathing assistance is required — or when a particular skin area needs to remain dry — the handheld offers good flexibility.

The main safety concern with a handheld is the way it is mounted for storage on the wall.

There are slide bars that are being manufactured as grab bars — even with small diameters — and these are great.

Look for such a slide bar with the ability to be used as a grab bar in an emergency because it will be used as such anyway — even if it's not designed or intended to be used that way — just because it is there.

Make sure it is anchored well into the wall.

Also, be careful that the hose is not a tripping hazard.

**Towel Bars/Hooks/Rings**

This is a major safety issue in bathrooms.

Just as slide bars for a handheld or personal shower are not designed to be used as grab bars unless specifically manufactured and installed for this purpose — in addition to their slider function — towel bars generally are not designed for this purpose either.

Nevertheless, many towel bars and rings — especially those installed near or inside the tub or shower space — are used as a grab bar in a panic.

When someone loses their balance and slips, they look for the first thing they can find to support their weight or break their fall.

The towel bar often is selected because it looks like it will work. Unfortunately, many towel bars will break when sufficient downward or gripping pressure is applied to them — such as during a panic fall — or they may pull lose from the wall.

They are only designed to support a few towels and not someone's full body weight as they are falling.

Even if the bars or rings don't actually break from the added pressure of someone trying to use them for support, they easily can pull lose from the wall. Either way, they will fail to support someone.

Nevertheless, there are towel bars designed to be used as grab bars also.

The important safety consideration is that when a towel is on the bar or rod, someone may grab it rather than the bar, and it may slip off the bar and defeat the intended purpose.

For overall safety, comfort and convenience, towel bars should be mounted away from the actual shower or bath area so that they are not mistakenly used for support.

Hooks for towels do not tend to keep the towels on them very well and can cause injury if someone falls against them.

They may also slip or trip on the towel that has fallen to the floor.

Rather than giving your customers an allowance to select their own towels bars, it is better if you install ones that you know will work properly — and ones you can stand behind with your warranty.

If you prefer, you can offer upgrades for different designs, finishes, styles, and colors. They just need to be anchored well into the wall in order to be effective.

## Strategic Grab Bars

People tend to associate grab bars in a residential setting with people requiring them due to age or a specific need.

Thus, you would not generally install them in new construction unless they were specifically selected as an upgrade by the customer.

However, they do serve a useful universal design function when used as a positive strategy.

I call this concept "strategic grab bars" or "safety grab (assist) bars."

I think for safety, comfort, and convenience, a well-designed, well-located, and attractive grab bar should be positioned and mounted vertically near the entrance to every tub or shower — at a suitable height for use by everyone in the household.

# Important Universal Design Strategies

It's likely that everyone at least once in their lifetime has needed a little extra support getting in or out of the tub or shower.

This could be because they slipped or lost their balance getting in or out of the tub or shower.

Perhaps they had an injury or recent surgery that kept them from putting their full weight on the ground, or they got a muscle cramp or spasm (in their leg, foot, or back) that interfered with their ability to stand or put their entire weight on their feet.

Maybe they were generally sore from exercise or other activity. Possibly it was the flu, a head cold, or sinuses.

So, using strategic grab bars (probably just one per application) is a good universal design feature that can be incorporated into an aesthetically pleasing look.

Along these same lines, replace all "pseudo-grab bars" you have been using with something that is specifically designed to provide the required support.

Remove towel bars and rings, soap dishes, toothbrush holders, or anything else in the bath or shower area that might be grabbed by someone for support in a panic situation that is not designed to provide such support, and replace them with ones that are designed to provide support for loss of balance or a fall.

Grab bars must be designed to hold up to the pressure and force applied to them, and they must remain anchored to the wall.

## Tilt-Out/Tip-Out Sink Front Bins

A space that usually goes unused that lends itself to a great universal design strategy in the kitchen and bathrooms is the cabinet blank in front of the sink — one or two depending on the design, and with or without dummy drawer pulls.

For convenience and efficiency, these can be turned into functioning tilt-out or tip-out storage bins or trays — depending on their depth. Otherwise, they remain unused storage potential.

Again, you are creating a memory point as well as something functional and useful.

These bins can be used in the kitchen and bath and will replace medicine cabinets in bathrooms. You can eliminate the medicine cabinets (if you typically include them) or offer them as an option.

They bring handy, everyday items right to your fingertips.

People of any age or ability can use these as they require very little effort to pull them down, don't latch but stay

# Important Universal Design Strategies

in place with tension hinges, and don't have a particularly large capacity so weight is usually not a concern.

The main safety concern would be keeping sharp items, medicines, and other dangerous items from such bins if there are young people living in the home or visiting the home — so remind your customers of this safety tip as you are showing the benefits of having the bins.

Point out to your customer that this is normally unused space that you have designed with their convenience in mind.

In designing your countertops, sinks, and cabinets, make sure there is enough room to employ this technique.

For undermount or integrated bowl sinks, check for available space between the cabinet and the edge of the sink bowl.

## Body Dryer

This feature is as high-tech, modern, and state-of-the-art as they come, but it is very efficient and a great universal design strategy.

It provides safety, comfort, convenience, and is highly accessible.

This is a heated, forced air, electric dryer for use after showering.

It is mounted in a corner of the shower and provides a series of heated air jets to blow dry anyone in front of it much the same way that hair dryers or automatic hand dryers do.

They are said to take about the same amount of time that a person uses to towel dry, but towel drying does not remove all of the water like these do.

For anyone with range-of-motion issues, someone who might need help drying themselves, or anyone who needs to make sure they get completely dry, this is a great idea. It can be used standing or seated.

It's also a great conversation starter when your owner's guests or friends see it. Plus, it is quite sanitary and saves on laundering towels.

This would be a great optional feature to offer so that just the people who wanted it could select it. It definitely will be a memory point for your customers.

## Toe-Kick Lighting

The toe kick — that little recess of a few inches tall by a few inches deep that keeps the base cabinets from resting directly on the floor and gives people a place to

Important Universal Design Strategies 85

put their feet to maintain their balance while in front of the cabinets — can be put to effective use with LED rope lighting, fluorescent strip lighting, xenon strip lighting, or LED strip lighting.

This provides additional indirect ambient lighting for the kitchen, bath, or laundry room — for safety or general illumination in an otherwise unused space.

It can be installed with a dimmer control if desired. It also can be switched, used with a timer or photo cell, or just left on because of its energy efficiency.

Since this is new construction, you can have it wired in place and not worry about finding a place to plug it in.

It makes a great night light and helps out in low-light situations when overhead or other lights are not on or available. It is inexpensive to use since it uses very little energy.

**Under-Cabinet/Task Lighting**

The kitchen requires a variety of lighting sources since there are so many different types of tasks going on there.

Again, like is the case for toe-kick lighting, this is taking advantage of an underutilized area of the kitchen, bath, or laundry room for additional lighting.

This provides more countertop, workspace, and indirect ambient lighting by mounting a light source under the upper cabinets.

It can be switched, used with a timer, or just left on because of its energy efficiency — LED rope lighting, fluorescent strip lighting, xenon strip lighting, or LED strip lighting.

It also makes a great night light and helps out in low-light situations when overhead or other lights are not on.

Your customers will be impressed with this noticeable and beneficial addition to the upper cabinets.

**Overhead Lighting**

At one time, homes were built with ceiling light fixtures in every room. While they often delivered harsh, localized lighting that could cast strong shadows and didn't fill the entire room with effective lighting, each room at least had this light source.

Some new construction still offers ceiling lighting fixtures, hanging lighting fixtures, or chandeliers in foyers, living rooms, dining rooms, bedrooms, kitchens, baths, hallways, stairways, laundry rooms, porches, patios, garages, and basements. You might already be doing this.

However, the light output is often insufficient for the activity in the room or space — making this a safety, convenience, and comfort issue.

Depending on the size, shape, and design of the lighting fixtures and the number and wattage of bulbs they can support, it may be possible to increase the light output.

Be aware of shadows and glare caused by overhead lights that may affect vision and depth perception and be a comfort and safety concern.

Increasing the bulb wattage or equivalence may be sufficient, but a new or additional light fixtures or source may be required as the solution.

The type of light bulbs available for consumers to use in ceiling fixtures has changed. Incandescent bulbs have been phased out. The CFL's (compact florescent bulbs) have safety, health, and practical concerns (sometimes they don't fit well or are unattractive) involved with using them.

Regular florescent tubes and rings (with less safety and health issues than CFL's but still some present) and halogen bulbs (although they produce a lot of heat) can still be used.

LED lighting is the trend of the future.

They tend to cost more initially but last several years, can be used with a dimmer, are being manufactured in higher wattage equivalent outputs, and are more widely available than they were.

In living rooms, dining rooms, family rooms, bathrooms, and bedrooms, wall lamps or sconces offer supplemental lighting but generally not enough to light a large area.

In kitchens and bathrooms, the toe-kick and under-cabinet or task lighting that I mentioned are great supplemental lighting sources.

Many ceiling fans come with light kits optional or already installed. This provides a central ceiling light resource also — with the same issues as ceiling mounted fixtures in terms of light output, harsh light, glare, and shadows.

**Ceiling Fans**

Ceiling fans are great for providing comfort and air circulation and often function as ceiling light fixtures.

You likely already include ceiling fans or make them available as an option in your homes.

Keeping lights and fans dusted (air quality and general appearance) and avoiding a strobing effect (with the

# Important Universal Design Strategies 89

fan creating a pulsing light pattern on the walls, ceiling, or floors) are the main issues with ceiling fans and the lights attached to them.

Make sure that these are not issues in your models and sales center, and remind your customers to keep the fans dusted regularly so that their indoor air quality is not affected.

In addition to being a light source that can be operated in conjunction with the fan or independently, ceiling fans themselves can provide addition comfort and convenience in a room and are a good universal design strategy.

For additional comfort and convenience, the fans can be regulated for speed (as well as downdraft or updraft), and the lights that are attached to them can be used with a dimmer control.

## Skylights

In any room where additional overhead lighting is desired — primarily during daylight hours — skylights are a good choice.

As long as they are installed properly so that there are no leaks and are not shadowed excessively by overhanging or blowing tree branches, skylights (when ceiling space and rafters accommodate or allow their use) can be an effective lighting source to contribute to overall safety, convenience, and comfort.

Also, they will reduce the energy demand for other lighting during daylight hours so there is an economic benefit as well for your customers.

Planning where they will go before finalizing your room sizes and trussing plan will help achieve the look and function you desire.

Skylights come in square and rectangular shapes with either flat or domed lenses — fixed or operational.

They also come round with polished steel tubes connecting a ceiling lens or diffuser with the roof lens (available in a variety of diameters and brands).

The round skylights also have light kits so that they can double as a ceiling light during evening hours or when supplemental lighting is needed.

## **Eye-Level Controls**

This is a universal design element that addresses accessibility, comfort, convenience, and safety issues in your home.

Often controls in a home, such as thermostats and ceiling fans switches — and sometimes even mixing or distribution valves in tubs and showers as well as digital displays and controls for wall ovens and microwaves — are mounted higher than a child, short adult, or person in a wheelchair could easily access and use.

However, regular light switches typically are located at a reasonable height.

Controls that are located generally less than 48" (4 feet) above the floor allow the widest range of accessibility and usage.

Thus, the small child or adult, those who might be in a wheelchair, those who might have physical limitations that keep them from standing erect (including those requiring support from a cane or walker), or those with range-of-motion issues in their elbows or shoulders that prevent a normal arm extension could reach them — in addition to those of average or above average height.

Eye level for a typical adult in a wheelchair is defined by the ADA as 51" — a smaller or larger person could experience a little variation in this number.

Still, other national standards (such as ADA which generally isn't a requirement for residences) call for controls to be no higher than 54" from the floor for a person in a wheelchair to reach if they are alongside and directly beneath it and no higher than 48" from the floor for them to reach if they are in front of and facing it.

This might be somewhat dependent on the length of someone's arm, but it seems to be a reasonable height for children and smaller adults also. Of course, "no higher than" means they can be lower.

If wall controls are placed in the general vicinity of light switches, they would be more convenient and aesthetically pleasing than having them take up more wall space.

In terms of safety and comfort, it's beneficial for more rather than fewer people in the home to be able to access and use these controls — including being able to read them and set them (the adjustable or programmable ones such as the thermostats) because they are at a comfortable height.

This can be emphasized during your sales presentation as a design choice that allows most anyone in the home to read and use the thermostat, fan switches, ovens, and other controls as well.

Then contrast this with the way most other new and existing homes have their controls located.

## Electrical Outlets

Depending on the building codes in effect where you are, the standard location of an electrical outlet from the floor is likely fine.

However, installing standard electrical receptacles higher than usual above the floor so they are in easy reach of everyone is a good universal design strategy — as long as they are not so high as to call attention to their placement.

In some rooms such as kitchens, bathrooms, and laundry rooms, the outlets tend to be higher anyway — just over the height of countertops or adjacent to them.

Sometimes, they are mounted in the sides of the base cabinets if they are accessible in the room.

In other rooms, such as bedrooms, outlets can be a little higher because furniture often hides them and makes them difficult to access when installed closer to the floor.

When the outlets are located higher than typically seen in rooms that do not have countertops, point out why that has been done and the benefits of having them more accessible.

Nevertheless, normal placement of outlets in homes is not totally inconsistent with the ADA guidelines (9" for direct access by a person in a wheelchair and 18" for someone reaching for it from a wheelchair position), but if they were a little higher, more people could reach them easier without bending so much.

This would include taller adults, people using a walker, people with range-of-motion issues, and those who have difficulty bending down or standing up again.

## **Wall-Mounted Mirrors**

All homes have mirrors — in bathrooms, bedrooms, living rooms, dining rooms, foyers, or hallways.

Many are decorative mirrors — regardless of their size or shape — that are framed and hung on the wall like a picture.

Some, such as in bathrooms, are large and mounted directly to the wall with adhesive or clips.

Others are considered to be "full-length" and attach to the back of a door.

Still others are used as bypass or bi-fold closet door panels.

The way that mirrors become a universal design concept and strategy is when they are accessible and usable by everyone in the home.

They don't necessarily have to be a tilted mirror that adjusts on a pivot (aiming somewhat downward with the top of the mirror being further from the wall that the bottom), but this can be a universal design treatment if everyone in the home can use the mirror comfortably and see themselves in it.

Generally, the height at which tilted or fixed mirrors are mounted and the focal length created by the installation (particularly with a tilted mirror) means that the mirrors are too high for people to see more than just their head and upper torso.

Mirrors mounted behind the sink are no lower than 30" when they rest right on a 30" counter; however, this conventional height for the bathroom sink is giving way to a 36" counter height. With a 4"-5" backsplash and an inch or so above that, and the bottom of the mirror is now 41"-42" or more above the floor.

Additionally, there usually there is a wall opposite from where the wall-mounted mirror is installed that keeps someone from backing up far enough to get a longer view.

Even when someone gets a full body view from a wall-mounted mirror, the distance is such that they are quite far from the mirror.

Then, being able to see much detail for grooming or choosing an outfit becomes an issue.

Lighting above or around the mirrors further affects the functionality of the mirrors due to glare, "hot spots," insufficient lighting, shadows, and the color temperature of the bulbs.

Full-length and closet door panels offer a much better solution than wall-mounted mirrors because they accommodate any physical size. A toddler, a person in a wheelchair, and a basketball player can all see themselves in such mirrors.

People can get as close as necessary to the mirror.

In selecting mirrors, pay attention to the weight of the mirrors relative to where they will be installed or used, the likelihood of the mirrors beginning to de-silver along the edges and creating warranty issues, and the general quality of the glass so imperfections are avoided.

All homes have mirrors, but you can stress how and why you have selected the mirrors for your customers as you have. You also can point out how existing homes and your competitors have not been so considerate in addressing their needs.

# 5

# Other Universal Design Strategies

## Additional Strategies For Safety, Convenience, Comfort And Accessibility

There are several other universal design strategies, treatments, and recommendations that can positively impact the overall quality of your customers' lives in the new homes you are creating for them.

The following suggestions, concepts, strategies, ideas, treatments, solutions, and designs can be added into a new home under construction or about to be built to make them more comfortable, safe, convenient, or accessible.

Some are going to have wider appeal than others, but all can be effective. Some might be dependent on your price point.

These strategies will require some advance planning and consultation.

They are more complex than just swapping out something that was planned or formerly used and replacing it with something else.

In some cases, major changes are involved.

The issue is not whether they apply to all ages and abilities but whether you want to incorporate them into the homes you are building — and to what extent.

## Contrast And Glare

As we age, our eyes are more affected by bright lights and glare. We are more susceptible to misjudging distances and determining how close objects are that might be in front of us.

Some people have more pronounced vision issues than others — regardless of age.

Therefore, two strategies that are effective for eliminating glare or confusion about surfaces and where objects are located are the use of color or contrast and using less shiny or reflective surfaces.

Glass (window glass, mirrors, glass panels in appliances, and glass shower enclosures — if you still

# Other Universal Design Strategies

use them) and hard surfaces such as countertops, appliance fronts (unless they have a matte finish), and ceramic, marble, concrete, and polished hardwood flooring are especially prone to reflecting light sources and creating glare when overhead lights are used. Sometimes natural light can do this also.

In kitchens, often a monochromatic look is used to be aesthetically pleasing, but it is not the best design for universal accessibility, safety, and comfortable use.

It needs to be obvious where countertops and floors are located and not have them just appear to blend from one surface to another.

A technique for defining countertops is something called "edge-banding" where a contrasting color is used on the edges of the countertops to show where the countertop surface begins.

Doing this with some hard surfaces such as granite or quartz will take more effort and will add to the cost. However, it will make the kitchen safer.

As for the flooring, toe-kick lighting will illuminate part of the floor to show its location relative to the cabinets and reduce glare as well.

Using red knobs on stove or cooktop fronts is a similar strategy, as is the one about adding a device to the end of faucets (when it will fit) that lights up blue for cold water and red for hot or using a faucet that displays a color for the relative temperature setting.

You can show your customers how you have taken into account potential glare and contrast issues and resolved or reduced them for greater safety.

Even when you are selling to a relatively young audience, they have older family members and potential visitors to take into consideration. Also, they may stay in the home for several years.

## **Flooring**

Flooring is a matter of personal choice, but there are types of flooring that tend to be more problematic than others for air quality, maintenance, accessibility, comfort, and safety.

Depending on the volume of homes you are building, you likely are looking for good value for your company in selecting flooring, but you also need to consider the value to the customer.

Thus, there are universal design choices and strategies concerning flooring.

In general, carpeting is not a good flooring choice anywhere in your homes even though builders typically include it in model homes, sales centers, and new construction. It's traditional, relatively easy to get and install, and not particularly expensive.

Also, it's part of the selection process and makes a nice trial closing question — choosing the pad and the color or style from the ones that are included or upgrading to something more substantial or available in more styles and colors.

Upgrades can be a profit source for you as well — but this is true for other flooring also.

As to how practical carpet is, when it gets wet from rain or snow tracked onto it or from outerwear, shoes, or umbrellas dripping onto it — or when the door is opened and the wind blows in the rain or snow — it tends to remain wet for a period of time.

Pets will track in the precipitation and dirt also.

Wet carpeting is more susceptible to attracting dirt and leaving noticeable dirty marks or stains that remain even after the area is dry.

It shows stains from food (especially ones with sauces, condiments, and gravies) and beverage spills (wine, fruit juice, Kool-Aid, coffee, tea, milk). It stains from pet accidents, blood from cuts, and anything else tracked or spilled onto it (oil, grease, mud).

In fact, a question that is often used asks home shoppers to contrast owning a new home with its brand new carpeting that hasn't been walked on yet versus a resale with used carpeting and an unknown history.

Now, you can reword this question to contrast used carpeting with a clean hard surface flooring that you are offering that is better to have than carpeting.

Besides, carpeting tends to off-gas, and it retains dirt and other pet and airborne allergens. More than other types of flooring, it develops noticeable wear patterns.

It presents air quality issues and typically needs replacing every few years. It also fades from the UV rays in sunlight and florescent lighting.

Carpeting needs constant vacuuming or shampooing and is never really showroom clean again.

Small, sometimes sharp, objects can fall into the carpet and be unnoticeable until stepped on.

People may be expecting to see carpeting in your homes because that's what every other builder offers. However, be sure to explain that you have their health, safety, comfort, convenience, and accessibility in mind — and that you have chosen to be a builder that provides flooring that is better in several respects for their well-being.

While aesthetically beneficial, area rugs are similar to carpeting and can be a slipping or tripping hazard — for basically anyone.

They hold dirt and allergens much the same way as carpeting, but they generally can be laundered more frequently.

To maintain true universal design, their use in the home would be disallowed for safety and accessibility. Keep this in mind in staging and decorating your sales center and models.

Hard surface flooring is the best to use, but hardwood flooring or hardwood-like flooring (engineered wood, laminates, and bamboo) should not be used in wet areas. Moisture causes the grain to expand and contract and affects the seams and joints.

Laminates and engineered wood flooring do not breathe so any water spilled on them will be trapped beneath them when it seeps through the joints and seams.

Bamboo is water resistant (not waterproof), but it is not recommended for use in areas where it could get wet.

Ceramic tile — especially the new reticulated tile that fits together tightly and requires very small to even no grout lines — is a hard surface that holds up well to water, spills, and foot traffic.

It is available in a variety of sizes and colors to match the color palette of the room in which it is installed and fit the proportions of the room. Upgrades in quality, style, and size are possible here also.

The main issue with ceramic flooring is safety — being slick or slippery when wet or too shiny — which creates glare or prohibits good traction for walking across safely or using an aid such as a cane or walker.

In these cases, treads of some type or a smaller tile or mosaic pattern that is inlaid in places will provide more traction.

Ceramic tile typically shows wear patterns less than other types of flooring.

Vinyl flooring has made a comeback.

It generally is well-accepted and comes in a variety of patterns and colors. It offers a little cushion so it is easier on the feet and legs when standing on it and comes in several sizes and installation options.

Another type of flooring material that seems to work well — especially in the kitchen — is the natural product cork, but it must be sealed frequently.

Cork is especially nice to stand on and helps to cushion dishes and glasses when they are accidentally dropped onto it. Consider this as an upgrade for kitchen areas.

What you give up in terms of carpeting as a selection option and profit center can be matched or even exceeded through ceramic tile, hardwood, bamboo, vinyl, and cork flooring choices.

## Automatic Dustpan

A central vacuum system is a great idea to have in the homes you build, but it is not purely a universal design feature. Nevertheless, this can easily be installed as an included or offered as an optional feature — depending on your price point.

It offers convenience as far as being able to plug the hose into various wall ports located around the home instead of moving an upright or canister vacuum cleaner around the house, but it still requires some physical size, strength, and coordination to be able to use it effectively.

However, once you have the central vacuum system, you can provide the automatic dustpan as part of it. This is a great universal design feature.

The automatic dustpan port is a station connected to the central vacuum that is installed at floor level in the baseboard (available in various finished and colors). It is activated by a foot switch.

One simply sweeps the floor with a broom or dustmop and moves the dust pile to the automatic dustpan where it is vacuumed away into the holding tank.

This is a universal feature because anyone capable of using a broom — even from a wheelchair or a walker — can sweep a pile of dust toward the automatic dustpan.

The switch on the port can be activated without bending down or touching it except by one's foot — or the broom handle or similar object that one could use to operate it.

This is a great memory point and another way to improve indoor air quality.

**Room-To-Room Transitions**

When two different types or thicknesses of flooring meet in a doorway — or between rooms even without a doorway — an uneven transition between the two surfaces results.

It can present safety, accessibility, and comfort issues.

Even with a molding strip between the two surfaces, going from one surface height (regardless of what it is) to another can present challenges for kids pushing toys along the floor, baby strollers, walkers, wheelchairs, and even furniture or carts on casters.

Walking from one surface to the other can even be a potential tripping or stumbling hazard for anyone who catches the heel of their shoe or their toe (wearing shoes or not) on the molding.

A uniform thickness of flooring — even if it's not exactly the same product throughout the home — is the safe and comfortable way to handle this issue.

By not having carpeting in the home, much of this issue will disappear.

## Motorized Shelving

Sometimes the height differential between members in a home is so great that solutions are sought for accommodating the location of shelving or countertops in closets, kitchens, and other areas where people can have access to them easily.

This is likely an optional solution — not for everyone and not for every budget.

However, it does provide the ability to accommodate a very wide range of individual users in a single household.

When people in a household have differing needs — because they range from tall to short, some are using assistance such as a wheelchair, some just prefer to sit when preparing meals or need to because of stamina or balance issues, or some prefer countertops and other surfaces at a lower or higher height than "normal" — motorized shelving can be a great choice.

It has the ability to bring many things to a comfortable height (up or down from a typical height) for the person desiring to use whatever it is that can be adjusted this way.

This is a universal feature because it is designed for convenience and comfort as much as it is for safety and accessibility.

This can be used in a closet to move items around on a track — or up and down — in a tight space, or just for convenience.

It can be used in the bath or powder room to allow access to literally anyone of any height or ability by moving a sink (vessel or one mounted in a small countertop) up and down as long as the water supply lines and drain tubing are flexible and installed with this in mind.

It can be used in the kitchen to provide comfortable and accessible eating space by moving a countertop up or down. It also can be used to raise or lower cabinets, shelving, cooktops, and sinks.

This can be included in higher-end or custom home s or offered as a creative design option to accommodate people who can benefit from it.

## Kitchen Islands

In homes where you include an island as a feature in the kitchen, some safety, convenience, and access issues need to be addressed.

Most of the islands that I have seen in new home designs or kitchen remodels are functionally too large for the kitchen floor space.

People like the idea of having an island, but quite often there simply is not enough space around the island for two people to be in the same area at the same time or for a cabinet or appliance door to be opened or accessed easily.

Sometimes it's difficult for even one person to navigate the space around the island.

There needs to sufficient clear space — generally 48"-60" — around each of the three or four sides of the island where cabinets, appliances, tables, passageways, or other functional areas of the kitchen are located.

It's not just a matter of someone in a wheelchair being able to move around the island easily. This is a matter of general access and function as well as comfort, convenience, and safety.

While wheelchair access is a consideration, it's a larger issue of two or more people — comfortably and safely — being able to be in the kitchen at the same time without bumping into each other, blocking the passageway, or interfering with what the other one is doing.

This would be true whether they are standing or seated.

Sometimes when the islands are really large for the kitchen space, it's tight for even one person to be in the kitchen and move around comfortably.

Thus, opening cabinet doors and drawers, using the oven or cooktop, opening the dishwasher, opening and using the microwave, preparing food, accessing the sink, and opening the refrigerator (or getting water or ice from the in-door dispenser) are actions that could go on simultaneously — or nearly so — with two or more people in the kitchen together.

People might not even be in the kitchen together for the same reason.

For instance, one person (or even more than one) might be eating or preparing a snack, getting a larger meal started, cleaning up from an earlier meal, washing dishes in the sink, putting dishes or groceries away, getting something to drink from the refrigerator, getting out pots or pans for meal preparation, washing their hands, making or getting a cup of coffee, reading the paper, or using their computer or tablet on the countertop — and the other person or persons could be doing a different one of these activities or even something else.

Regardless of the size of the island — after it is adjusted to fall within acceptable clearance distances — all of the corners should be rounded with a radius sufficient to prevent injury from accidentally running into it while walking past or falling against it.

For universal design, if the resulting island is large enough for someone to sit down at it and eat — rather than just being a food preparation area or serving station — part of the countertop should be low enough and open enough to allow people to sit (or pull up a wheelchair or a regular height dining chair) and eat.

In such cases, remember to mark the edges of the countertop to show that they are at different heights.

Not every kitchen is large enough to accommodate an island, but if you want to include one, make sure the kitchen is large enough to support one in the style and size you have in mind. Otherwise, skip the island.

You can tell your customers exactly what I have told you here.

Your competitors who offer islands likely have them too large to be functional in the overall kitchen space.

## Modular Sink Base Cabinets

While having roll-in or roll-under access to the kitchen or bathroom sinks is often desired, not everyone needs it. For this reason, it's not recommended as a universal design feature.

Nevertheless, as both a universal design and adaptable design feature, sink base cabinets in the kitchen and bathrooms can be designed and created intentionally to be removed later on as necessary — to create a more open look or to allow wheelchair access.

While this likely is not your concern unless you are a custom builder and this is specifically requested, you can have the cabinets created as modular units so that the kitchen base cabinet could be taken out at later time (with those on either side of it remaining in place) to allow full access for someone in a wheelchair or just more open space for use with a chair or bench.

The removable, modular sink base cabinet would be a unit entirely separate from the rest of the cabinetry that can be installed along with the cabinets on either side of it but removed later without affecting the integrity of the remaining cabinets or countertop.

It is universal because it shows no outward sign of being any different from the other cabinets at present, but it is easily adaptable when the time comes for a fully accessible sink by simply removing the modular sink base unit.

Of course, there are other solutions for creating wheelchair or sit-down access at the sink by removing the cabinet doors and cabinet floor or designing them to be retracted — or by using a wall hung sink or a pedestal sink in the bathrooms.

## Retractable Sink Base Cabinet Doors

While a modular sink base cabinet can be installed to be removed at a later date to provide wheelchair access to a sink, a universal design solution rather than an adaptable one is to create retractable doors on the sink base cabinet.

Whenever someone needs to access the sink from a wheelchair — or use it from a seated position (for stamina or just convenience) — the doors on the cabinet can be created to retract on a track or groove along the inside walls of the cabinet much like the doors on a TV cabinet or entertainment center used to do.

It may not even be necessary to remove the toe-kick, but if that is desired, there are two way to handle this.

The toe-kick for this base cabinet can be removed and left off so that when the doors are open and used in the retracted position, the place where the toe-kick normally would be is empty.

The cabinet floor also can be hinged and folded back inside the cabinet (with the toe kick riser either coming with the floor or remaining in place).

If the toe-kick moves with the cabinet flooring, it can be moved out of the way when cabinet access is desired — even if the doors are just opened and not retracted.

With this method, the outward appearance is the same whether or not the cabinet is designed for wheelchair access — instead of having a noticeable missing toe-kick.

Another solution is to remove the floor entirely or partially — with the toe-kick being removed as well.

It could be reconfigured and installed as a plumbing access panel (when needed) on a slant to provide open floor space in front of it, conceal the plumbing behind it, and have open shelves on it for storing cleaning products and paper goods.

The doors would need to be kept from moving past their flush closed position when not retracted.

This is not something that you would install or offer routinely, but knowing that you can provide such a solution gives you more flexibility in addressing the needs or desires of your customers.

## Cabinets And Drawers

Cabinets are a big focus of universal design because they are used in many rooms throughout the home, and storage is something everyone needs. They aren't limited to just the kitchen or the bath.

There are several universal design strategies involving upper and base cabinets — beyond what I already mentioned about the pulls, the tilt-out/tip-out bins, the toe-kick lighting, task lighting, and the modifications to the sink base cabinets.

Many of these opportunities can be optional — giving you some versatility and flexibility in meeting the needs and demands of your home shoppers, differentiating yourself from other builders in your marketplace, and creating additional revenue streams for your company.

Some of these strategies you may not choose to offer, but you should be aware of them nonetheless.

There really are two main issue concerning cabinets: accessibility and ease of use.

In the cabinets you select for inclusion in your base package in the kitchen, bathrooms, basement, laundry room, linen closet, bedroom closets, garage, summer kitchen, mud room, patio, home office, dining room, hallways, or wherever else they are located in the home, look at the size of the doors and drawers, the physical weight of the doors and drawers, the flexibility of using the storage space, the location of the door or drawer pulls on the actual doors or drawers, and the amount of room in front of them for someone to access them.

Ease of retrieving items that are stored is a big issue.

With drawers or pull-out shelves, bins, or baskets, the suspension system needs to provide sufficient support for the weight and easy movement of the drawers, shelves, bins, or baskets in and out — whether they are empty or loaded to capacity.

Thus, they should not be dependent on someone of any particular size, strength or ability being able to use them.

They should work equally well whether they are being accessed by someone from a standing, seated, or kneeling position.

## Other Universal Design Strategies

This certainly can be conveyed to your customers during your sales presentation and contrasted with builders who do not take this into account.

To appeal to everyone in the household — regardless of their age, size, or ability — a good design idea for ultimate storage efficiency is to approach it much the same way that we want the controls to be located in the home.

You'll recall that the guidelines are for them to be located 4½ feet (54") or less from the floor with an even better objective keeping them no higher than 48".

Obviously, cabinets are taller than that and can go all the way to the ceiling, but they should be designed so that most of the commonly used items are easily accessible and retrievable at eye level or below.

Certainly one strategy is to install upper cabinets actually resting on the countertop.

While this concept makes them more accessible, it takes away useable counterspace that must be accounted for and accommodated elsewhere in the room.

An island — if the dimensions of the kitchen and intended size of the island permit it to be used — can be a solution.

An alternative is to mount one or more upper cabinets lower than their traditional height but still up from the countertop a few inches — making them easier to reach than at their traditional height and preserving some countertop functionality.

As I mentioned in discussing closet doors, another good idea is to look for smaller doors and cabinets so that a floor-to-ceiling linen, pantry, or supply cabinet can actually have two or more separate compartments rather than a very tall closet-like cabinet — that comes with a necessarily heavier, larger, and harder to control door.

Some designers and consumers are returning to an open-look where just open wall shelves are used for storing cups, glasses, and dishware — in place of cabinets.

There may or may not be upper cabinets used in conjunction with this design.

The openness certainly enhances accessibility. Safety may be more of a concern as objects could fall or be knocked from the shelves.

Along this same line, open cabinets are being used that have no doors on them. Again, access is enhanced, but knocked items from the cabinet or having them fall out may present safety concerns.

In thinking about whether to use these open designs, look at your research about market acceptance or see if you just want to offer it to see how it works.

You might offer it as a money-saving option for budget-conscious consumers who can live without the cabinets and use the credit for other items.

## Kitchen Desk

This is a great universal design concept that is often designed into a kitchen layout anyway.

Use it to your advantage because it has multiple uses for a variety of ages and abilities.

It is a sit-down desk that can be installed inline in a base cabinet run or separately along another wall in the kitchen — as a standalone or with other base cabinets and often with upper cabinets or shelving.

Traditionally this was presented as a "recipe desk," but it has so many more applications as the more universal "kitchen desk."

However, the kitchen area may need to be enlarged or reconfigured to allow the use of the kitchen desk.

The desk can be entirely open with just a countertop covering the space, or it can have a single desk drawer beneath the countertop or two or more adjacent drawers (depending on the width of the opening (knee space).

It can also have one or two of the drawer base cabinet units on either or both sides of the knee space much like a traditional desk.

The countertop can be the same height as the other countertop space in the kitchen, but it is more versatile at a lower height in the 30" range — or even at the 29" typical desktop height.

This lower height would be the recommended design to indicate that it is an intentional design element and that it can be used in multiple ways.

Since this is a fairly common feature in many kitchens, the design does not suggest anything unusual, and it fits right in.

Still, it allows wheelchair access as well as the ability for anyone else in the household (including kids doing their homework) to use this space.

It can be designed, used, or merchandised as a computer or TV/movie/gaming station (with a TV, desktop computer, notebook, or tablet) or just remain an open countertop for crafts, writing, meal planning, eating, meal or baking preparation (where doing it from a seated position is necessary or desired), cooking with a small appliance (coffee maker, crockpot, toaster oven, microwave, or induction burner) at a lower counter height, or several other uses where a desktop is beneficial because of its height, openness, and accessibility.

It certainly can accommodate wheelchair access and be used without any adaptation.

Be sure to point out the many uses and versatility of this space.

## **Sit-Down Vanity**

This is similar in design and concept to the kitchen desk and has been used in the master bathrooms of many homes for years.

It has never gone out of style, but its popularity seems to rise and fall in new construction.

Like the kitchen desk, the sit-down vanity can be installed inline in a vanity base cabinet run or separately along another wall in the bath — as a standalone.

Also like the kitchen desk, the sit-down vanity can be entirely open with just a countertop covering the space, or it can have one or more desk drawers immediately under the countertop (depending on the width of the opening — knee space).

It can even be built to look like a desk with vertical drawer units installed along one or both sides of the knee space.

As a universal design feature, the sit-down vanity, which is typically installed in the master bathroom (or occasionally in a dressing area near the bath), can also be used in the guest or secondary bathrooms for children or guests to use for their grooming needs.

A typical desktop height is 29" and many bathroom vanities are built to this height. They range all the way to 36".

Some people like the sit-down portion of the vanity to be at the same height as the rest of the bathroom base cabinets, while others prefer it to be slightly to definitely lower.

While the height of the sit-down vanity can vary, the concept of the sit-down portion itself is a nice universal design feature that is widely used.

Many of your customers will be expecting to see this feature.

### Up-Front Controls

Washing machines, laundry sinks, ranges, garbage disposals, range hoods, exhaust fans, dishwashers, cooktops, microwaves, ovens, and other appliances and fixtures in the home should be as accessible and usable by as many people as possible.

Therefore, the operating controls (including faucet handles where applicable), the digital displays, and everything else connected with operating the appliances and fixtures need to be located on the top surface of the appliance or fixture (at the front edge) or preferably on the front of the appliance, fixture, or device.

Look for and specify appliances that already are created this way — such as the front-loading washing machine, dishwasher, clothes dryer, and induction cooktop.

This is a great selling feature for your customers. It eliminates unnecessary reaching, avoids possible injury, and makes them accessible to everyone.

## Easy-Access Appliances

Kitchen and other major appliances are used in the home every day so we need to look at making them more accessible and useable by everyone in the household.

The appliances that come to mind that have great solutions already available are washing machines, refrigerators, cooktops, ranges, and dishwashers.

Others, such as ovens, clothes dryers, and microwaves, need to be selected or installed with universal design and accessibility in mind.

The front-loading washing machine has the controls and the door located on the front so that anyone can use it. It can even be raised with a pedestal base if it needs to be a little higher for members of the household.

A top loading washing machine does not provide these advantages and tends to be less energy efficient.

Refrigerators have two styles that offer great accessibility — the side-by-side and the french-door models.

In the french-door or armoire style with two doors (often equally sized) that close to the middle and open outward in either direction, the top shelves are going to be harder for someone short, seated, or with limited range or motion to reach.

However, there are models available with either two separate bottom drawers or with a drawer within a drawer.

Often one of these drawers has the option of serving as a refrigerator compartment in addition to being set as a freezer. Set to the refrigerator mode, access would be available for people unable to reach higher shelves in the refrigerator.

## Other Universal Design Strategies 125

There are many possibilities here for offering optional models to suit the needs, desires, and budgets of your customers.

Some cooktops have the controls on the surface along the front edge or in the lower corner of them. Induction cooktops have the touch controls along the front edge but on the surface of the cooktop.

Ranges (gas and electric) have their controls on the front facing out so they are easily accessible. Some knobs are actually red.

Dishwashers are accessible to all — either the traditional model with the door opening down and the pull out baskets or the newer style with two drawers that open independently. They work as well at their normal height for someone in a wheelchair or seated.

Again, you have some flexibility here in what you include versus what you offer as options.

As for appliances that need to be selected or installed with accessibility in mind, the oven when it is part of a range is fine. When the oven is mounted in the wall apart from the stove or range, it needs to be at a useable height — especially the controls and display.

Finding and selecting an oven with a side-opening door (hinged along the side rather than the bottom) provides more safety, convenience and accessibility than one that opens down. Just be aware of extra clearance that may be required for the door to open safely.

For double ovens, the top unit tends to be quite high for many people. Care should be taken to lower it and to make sure the controls and display are at eye-level or below.

Some newer clothes dryers have the controls mounted on the front, but many still have them at the back.

Microwaves are often mounted over the range in line with the cabinets. They typically have a range hood/exhaust fan and light function built into them also.

Because of where they are installed, they are difficult for many people to reach and use — especially reaching over a stove or cooktop that could be in use or being able to see the controls well due to the height of them.

People who are short, or those with range-of-motion or arm strength issues, face the additional challenge of removing hot food from the microwave and trying to set it down safely.

Some microwaves are installed resting directly on the countertop. While this brings them to a very useable and accessible level, countertop space is often forfeited.

## Wall Blocking

Wall blocking by itself — adding dimensional lumber (2" x 6", 2" x 8", 2" x 10", or 2" x 12") horizontally and flush (with the wide flat side to the front) between the vertical wall studs to provide material into which to anchor a future installation of grab bars or other devices — is not a universal design strategy.

However, it is an adaptable strategy that will facilitate the later installation by your homeowners of towel bars, grab bars, or other items that need to be anchored securely to the wall without being concerned about locating a stud or working with products that may not fit exactly where the studs are located — or needing to rely on wall fasteners.

The wider the boards you use, the more flexibility in choosing an appropriate future mounting height.

Using plywood sheathing (⅝" or ¾") across the studs will work, but it doesn't provide the thickness of 2" lumber and reduces the functional size of the room by its thickness since the drywall needs to go on top of it rather than applied directly to the wall studs as is the case with dimensional lumber blocking.

Hallways, baths, and kitchens would be typical installations, but laundry rooms, bedrooms, and other areas of the home could be feasible also.

Wall blocking may be something you decide to offer and then convey as a great benefit to your consumers, or it can be an available upgrade you offer.

## **Windows**

You select windows for your homes for a variety of reasons.

You look at how well they add natural light to a space, on their ability to provide ventilation and fresh air when opened, for the view they afford from various rooms, for how they might suggest furniture placement in a room (in a bedroom, family room, living room, dining room, or kitchen), and for the way they fit into the exterior design.

Windows generally are not selected for how accessible they are or how easy to open they are once cabinetry or furniture is in front of them — blocking them or creating a barrier to accessing them.

The issues are the general height of windows from the floor and the way they open.

How far someone might need to reach, how much hand and arm strength they may need, or the range-of-motion required to push the window sash open or operate the crank are additional considerations that may not immediately come to mind.

Depending on what your local building codes require as a minimum height of a window from the floor, windows that provide easy viewing through them from a seated position are at a good height for everyone.

At such a height, anyone can access them as well for egress in an emergency and for emergency personnel to gain entry.

This attribute of windows is often overlooked.

Thus, a relatively low window — in terms of distance of the sill from the floor — is a universal design feature because anyone can see through the glass and observe what is happening or enjoy the view.

The lower the windows are in relation to the floor, the easier they are going to be to open, but it's not just a matter of reaching the crank or the sash.

For safety, security, peace-of-mind, and comfort, the windows also need to be latched securely.

On single-hung and double-hung windows, the latching/locking mechanism is on top of the lower window sash or frame.

For casement windows, the latch that secures the windows (in addition to the crank) is usually located along the side of the window. Look for and select windows with the latch near the bottom or actually along the bottom rather than halfway up the side of the sash.

Depending on the size of the windows, how high they are installed from the floor, how heavy they are, and how difficult they are to open and close, a short person, a child, someone in a wheelchair, someone with range-of-motion issues in their upper body, or someone without a lot of hand and arm strength may be unable to release or operate the windows.

The actual ease of opening the window once it is unlatched is important also — turning the crank to open a casement window or raising the lower sash of a single- or double-hung window.

The single-hung and double-hung windows while commonly used are much less user-friendly than the casement windows.

Unlike the single- or double-hung windows, the casement windows also can be left somewhat open during a rain.

Taking these functional issues into account when designing your homes can translate into huge benefits for your customers and provide memory points while differentiating you from the competition.

Adding impact resistant glass will be beneficial and

universal also for safety and convenience — and peace of mind against possible intruders, mischief, vandalism, or wind storms.

## Elevators

Elevators are in a class by themselves.

They aren't what we typically think of as a universal design feature, concept, or strategy, and they don't apply to ranch-style or single-level homes unless there is a basement.

Nevertheless, in multi-level homes they can be used by people that don't climb stairs well or by anyone else. In that sense, they are universal.

With two-story homes (or more), there may be a great opportunity for adaptable design by creating an elevator shaft for future use.

Design your homes in such a way that, in at least one location in the home, a bedroom or hallway closet on each floor is situated one on top of the other.

It needs to be large enough to hold an elevator car so be sure to plan for this.

Then, if and whenever an elevator is desired, simply remove the ceiling of the first floor closet (which is the floor of the second floor closet) to create a cavity or shaft to house the elevator.

Make sure that the landing and approach room is sufficient to operate the elevator.

The ceiling/floor that is being removed would be designed in such a way that it could be taken out for this purpose.

The closet doors can remain, but they should not interfere with getting on or off the elevator.

Even when it's not possible to align the two closets to create an elevator shaft, an elevator still might be a safety, comfort, convenient, and accessible design choice that you would find space for in a custom design and install wherever it seemed feasible.

There also are elevators that can be installed outside the structure and attached and finished in such a way as to give the appearance that the home was designed and built with that feature included.

There are free-standing tubular elevators that can be used in spaces where a larger elevator wouldn't work or when a solution is desired without a lot of construction.

There are different primary energy sources available for elevators, but look for back-up batteries or how the unit can be powered by a back-up generator when there is a power outage.

This can be a good revenue source for you in providing the aligned closets or in the actual elevator installation, and they are less expensive to install in new construction than later — a good selling feature.

## Chair Lifts

Like the elevator, a chair lift only applies to two-or-more-story homes or ones with a basement to provide an alternative for moving people between floors.

The chair lift substitutes for the stairs or makes climbing them unnecessary while your owners can still go up or down a floor.

Chair lifts themselves are not a universal design feature. Neither are platform lifts for people who need to be transported between levels (or even from the outside to the entrance of your model or their home) while remaining in their wheelchairs.

Nevertheless, installing a chair lift may be desirable for someone who has moderate mobility, stamina, breathing, or balance issues.

Still, an electric outlet located at the base of the stairs and the landing — even if not required by the building code — will mean that a chair lift could be installed at a future date if necessary or desired.

In the meantime, one can never have too many outlets. An outlet located here would facilitate plugging in decorative holiday lights and using the vacuum or other electrical appliances in this area of the home.

Just make sure that sufficient floor space around the base of the stairs is maintained to accommodate the chair lift track. It typically rests on the floor and extends well past the base of the stairs.

Wall blocking inside and along the wall where a track might be installed at a later date would be a good use of adaptable design also.

The blocking can be an included or optional feature that you offer.

**First-Floor Master**

Obviously, this applies to multi-story homes and townhomes.

As people age, climbing stairs becomes more of an issue for a number of different reasons, such as range-of-motion, arthritis, deteriorating joints, old sports injuries that affect knees and other joints, balance, stamina, coordination, and cardio-vascular function.

Make sure to offer some of your floor plans with a first-floor or main-floor master suite.

The market is very receptive to this idea — even if it is not currently something your home shoppers need for themselves.

You will lose sales if you don't provide this in some, if not all, of your floor plans.

People might have elderly parents visit them who could benefit from a bedroom on the main floor. From time-to-time, illnesses, surgeries, or injuries may affect members of the household, and going up the stairs to their bedroom may not be feasible or easy.

In terms of resale value, having a first-floor master is vital. In ranch-style or one-level homes, this is not an issue, but it is essential in two-story homes.

Create a first-floor master or the ability to convert a den, study, play room, or family room into a master at a later date — with the adjacent full bath already there (not a hall bath but one specifically for that room).

## Back-Up Power

Storms happen in all parts of the country that can disrupt electrical power — from a few seconds to several hours or days.

While comfort, convenience, accessibility, and safety are important considerations during a power outage due to such items as alarm systems, lighting (interior and exterior), heating and air conditioning, computers, TVs, appliances, and refrigeration, some medically necessary equipment may depend on electricity as well.

Back-up generators are quite useful and universal for supplying electrical power needs when the normal power service is interrupted. They can be small or portable generators that will offer some supplemental power, but a larger, more permanent solution may be desired.

Installing whole-house generators means that they can take over the entire energy load of the home and ease any fears of going without essential and necessary systems, appliances, and other items in the home during an outage.

If chair lifts, platform lifts, or elevators are present in a home because you sold and installed them — or you provided for their future installation — they likely have back-up power designed into them. If not, the back-up generator would operate them.

Even a UPS (uninterruptible power supply) battery like we for our computers can provide temporary backup for a few uses of a power bed or chair lift. Be sure to mention this to your customers.

While everyone can benefit from having back-up power from a correctly installed generator that protects your homeowners and the power company employees from shock or back-feeds, not everyone may want to pay for having it.

You can offer it as an included feature and adjust your base price accordingly to cover it — and really elevate yourself above your competition — or you can offer it as an option in a couple of different sizes.

## Indoor Air Quality

Many people suffer from allergies, and there is more attention being paid to indoor air quality — particularly as the building envelop is being designed and created to be tighter.

Using low- or no-VOC paints, glues, adhesives, and building materials — or ones that don't off-gas — are being requested by an increasing segment of the population.

Eliminating carpeting, as I mentioned, is a positive step in improving indoor air quality because of the way it's made and the way it traps and hold dust and allergens.

I already mentioned the automatic dustpan port also.

Built-ins are attractive, but they are dust-catchers.

Niches, bookcases, open beams, large window sills and ledges, decorative columns with fluted surfaces, and many other building accessories and finishes add aesthetically to a home's interior but also present indoor air quality issues in terms of attracting dust or allowing dust to settle and remain on them.

They aren't always the easiest to vacuum or wipe off either.

I'm not talking about someone's personal furniture — that's their business.

I'm talking about built-in features that you include or add that contribute to dust accumulation and allergen retention in the living space.

A cleaner, easier-to-maintain look will promote better indoor air quality (while possibly sacrificing some aesthetic treatments), and your customers will appreciate that you have done this for them — especially as you point it out to them and differentiate yourself from your competitors.

# 6

# Universal Design On The Outside

## Why Look At The Exterior?

In addition to all of the modifications and changes you can make to your designs on the inside to help them sell and to be more desirable to a wider range of consumers — in terms of universal accessibility, safety, security, convenience, visitability, and comfort — there are many ways to improve the exterior of your homes as well.

This applies whether it's a single family detached home or a semi-attached/detached home such as a duplex, villa, or townhome.

Before someone ever gets inside their home, they need to be able to approach it safely and comfortably on the outside of it.

The same is true for your model homes, available homes that you show to your customers, and your sales center.

The principles of universal design and accessibility don't just magically begin once someone opens the front door and enters their living space.

They begin at the curb and continue along the entry sidewalks and driveway to the front door.

Often the curb appeal affects how someone feels about looking inside the home.

Here are a few ideas to get you started creating an accessible and safe living environment from the outside-in.

## Zero-Step/Barrier-Free Entrances

In some parts of the country, building codes may not allow a true zero-step entrance into the home that is at grade level.

However, there may other ways to accomplish this.

A gentle sloping or ramping that invisibly bridges the few inches that the threshold needs to be above grade for flooding concerns or other issues will create a similar effect.

Nevertheless, whatever the local building codes require or allow in terms of letting you create a zero-step threshold or entry — or prohibiting you from doing so — must be followed.

However, the concept of a zero-step or barrier free entry allows anyone easy, unrestricted access to your homes.

This would apply to your home shoppers, your homeowners, their guests, their visitors (invited or not), service personnel, delivery people, and anyone else approaching the home.

It would include basically anyone from young to old, those walking unaided, anyone using a walker or wheelchair (or other mobility assistance), those being pushed in a baby carriage or stroller, kids using a wheeled toy, or people with a range-of-motion or joint stiffness issue that makes stepping up and down difficult.

Regardless, everyone will need to step on or over the wooden or metal threshold against which the entry door closes.

Still, the concept of a barrier-free entry is to reduce and eliminate other steps and obstacles along the entry walk — from the driveway or street to the actual entrance of the home.

In some cases, an attractive, well-constructed, and well-landscaped ramp may be used as universal access to the home — or used in addition to steps or another type of approach that might be present.

This would provide an alternative entry without necessarily calling attention to the design or its presence and may be used whether they are required for accessibility or not.

This could be a profitable design option that you could offer your customers rather than something that it seemed you were not prepared to address.

An easy access entry presents added comfort, convenience, and accessibility to your homeowners.

**<u>Lighting</u>**

In Chapter 3, I mentioned photo cells, timers, and motion sensors.

These all work outside as well as indoors provided they can withstand the elements or are used in a relatively dry or covered area (such as on a porch or covered entry, or under the eaves or overhang).

Another type of lighting that can be used outdoors successfully and effectively is a solar powered light fixture.

It can be a yard or house light that stays on all night or one that just comes on when it detects motion — depending on what type of light is selected and what the objective is.

The principal advantage to this type of light is that it can be located anywhere on the property because it does not need to be wired into or plugged into electricity.

It can be as far away from the house or an electrical source as it needs to be to provide lighting for the residents.

It draws its energy from batteries that are recharged by the sun.

Of course, the solar collector that recharges the batteries needs to be in a place where it can receive sunlight.

When you install it on your models or sales center, be sure to locate it away from tree branches or other objects that might block the sunlight from reaching the solar collector.

This can be an included or optional feature by offering the benefit of additional security, safety, comfort, and peace-of-mind. Your competitors likely will not be offering this.

### Entry Shelves/Tables/Furniture

A universal design strategy that definitely appeals to all ages and abilities and addresses the major areas of safety, comfort, convenience, and accessibility is an outdoor entry shelf or piece of furniture such as a table.

Furniture is more a matter of personal taste, but you might find something fairly generic to use.

You can, and should, merchandise your models with this feature and create a great memory point and interest in that particular model before you even enter it with your customers.

As a shelf (or table or bench), this can be installed on every new home you build as an included feature right next to the entrance (the latch side or door handle side of the front door).

Install it or locate it on the wall of the home slightly below the door handle so as not to interfere with anyone approaching the door or with the safe operation of the door handle.

You can use most any dimension that you like, but it should be large enough and deep enough to be functional without be so big that it is obtrusive or a barrier to entering safely.

Depending on its size and shape, it might provide storage space inside or underneath it or allow for a small sculpture or plant on top.

It can be wood or metal and painted, stained, or decorated to be compatible with the general design, theme, style, and colors of the home or entry porch.

From time-to-time, if not most of the time, all of us get out of our cars and approach the entrance of our homes with our hands full of various things — the mail, groceries, packages, an umbrella, a jacket that we aren't wearing, shopping bags, books, tools, dry cleaning, a briefcase, purse, toddlers, a cup of coffee or a soft drink, fast food (that we are still eating or in the bag to eat once inside), or a cell phone.

Maybe we are trying to assist someone else to get into the home or show attention to a pet that greets us.

Then, with our hands full of whatever we are carrying or attending to, we need to look for our house keys, make or take a phone call, keep from dropping something we have been carrying that is beginning to slip, or have a hand free to open the door.

Having a shelf or object (such as a table or stand) to set things on makes perfect sense rather than trying to juggle them, balance them, setting them on the ground, or losing control and dropping them.

Your customers should appreciate this added and unusual detail for their comfort, safety, and convenience.

Just make sure that whatever you decide to use — a shelf, cabinet, stand, table, or other object or piece of furniture —that it is painted or otherwise treated to withstand precipitation if it is in an area that might get wet (directly or from windblown rain or snow).

## **Covered Entry/Guttering**

This is a safety, comfort, and convenience feature that definitely applies to all ages and abilities.

When people arrive at their front door — or have guests or visitors that come to their front door — it should be dry even if it is snowing or raining right up until the moment they arrive at the door.

People need to be sheltered from rain or snow when it is present so they can pause in a dry area immediately before entering their home (or one they are visiting) without being subjected to the precipitation.

This gives them time to compose themselves as they shake off the rain or snow, take off their raincoat, clean off their boots or shoes, or shake off and fold up their umbrella — whether they first have to unlock the door or just open it and enter.

Most entrances have an overhang of sorts, but at a minimum guttering should be installed to keep the precipitation from running off the roof and onto people — generally at a fairly heavy flow — when they approach the door.

Guttering also — if it is installed correctly — will collect and drain the water away from the sidewalk or driveway that people will use to approach the front door.

This will help keep everyone's feet dryer and provide safer, surer footing on the walkway and more accessibility without having to navigate around puddles or slippery spots on the walkway.

Many builders include guttering along the front of the home or over the entrance. Here are a couple of practical reasons on why it should be done that you can share with your customers.

Another is that it will help keep precipitation from entering the home when the front door is opened.

A covered entry or porch (that also has guttering along the edge of it for the reasons just mentioned) provides even more protection and shelter.

Then with the entry shelf, stand, table, or other piece of furniture I mentioned, people can set down anything they are holding while they open the door.

## Radiant Heating

In areas where temperatures are cold enough for ice and snow to be present, a universal design feature and treatment that provides safety, comfort, convenience, and accessibility is radiant heating.

Install this in the concrete sidewalks (front, back, and side), driveways, and patios around the home so that the ice and snow are melted and the possibility of slipping or having unsure footing is greatly reduced or eliminated.

This also will keep wet patches of melted snow or ice or other precipitation (rain or sleet) from freezing when the temperature drops low enough.

This can be a tremendously important and valuable feature that you can include in the base price of your homes or offer as an optional one, depending on how you want to position your product.

Either way, this feature is sure to be appreciated for the comfort, convenience, safety, and accessibility it offers.

## Unloading/Landing Area

Depending on how people use their two-car driveways, the surfaces often are large enough and sufficiently wide to accommodate people unloading from a vehicle without them stepping off the driveway and onto the grass, dirt, or planting area.

Generally, this would only be true if the vehicle was parked to the left side of the driveway with the right side being used for the loading area.

For driveways less than double-car in width, this universal design solution should be implemented.

However, for increased safety, convenience, comfort and accessibility, the driveway — regardless of the typical width you have been using — should be enlarged along its right side (facing it from the street).

This allows plenty of hard-surface footing for anyone to disembark from the vehicle (wherever it is parked on the driveway) and to allow plenty of space for a walker or wheelchair to be unloaded, set up, and used.

This strategy works in reverse for people entering a vehicle to have sufficient room to board the vehicle (with or without a wheelchair) and is appropriate for your home shoppers, your homeowners, and their visitors and guests.

The extra loading and unloading space is beneficial for everyone — especially on inclement days or when the vehicle needs to be loaded with luggage, supplies, schoolwork, pets, or other objects in addition to the occupants of the vehicle. The same holds true for unloading.

For vans with ramps or lifts that extend from the vehicle (to allow people in wheelchairs or those with other mobility issues to safely enter and exit the vehicle), there needs to be space for the ramp or lift to deploy and for people to still be on a hard surface while entering or after leaving the van.

This would apply to your homeowners and anyone else who needed the assistance of a ramp or lift assisted van.

When not needed for passenger unloading or loading, the extra driveway space can be used for parking (cars, motorcycles, golf carts, or bicycles), as a seating or gathering area with lawn chairs, or as a play area.

The extra width can be just as practical when not needed for getting in and out of the vehicles which is why this is a universal design and visitable strategy.

Be sure to point out to your home shoppers why this is such an important feature and why you have chosen to proactively include it for them.

Your competition won't offer it, and the difference will be noticeable to your customers.

## Sidewalks

Many new homes are designed and built without much attention to the sidewalks leading from the street to the front door or from the driveway to the front door.

A basic walkway is formed and poured according to the prevailing building code or site plan, and that is about it.

If your homebuyers have been looking at older homes also, they will have seen or be familiar with a variety of sidewalks in various conditions.

Sometimes a basic walkway is formed and poured — or one is created with brick pavers — without much attention to function.

Some homes don't even have a formal sidewalk — they just have a path, with or without stepping stones. The dirt path can become muddy, and those with stepping stones can become overgrown with grass and difficult to use because of the spacing between them or the fact that they are broken or pitched in various directions.

Some walkways have intermediate steps and may or may not have railings for assistance.

Thus, consider a much more strategic — and visitable — approach to the sidewalk where it is created wide enough for easy use by children playing, for people using a walker or wheelchair, for moving furniture or equipment in and out of the home, or for two or more people to walk side-by-side (together or coming and going) on the walkway.

With function in mind, width is important, but so is the quality of the surface footing (non-slip under most conditions), the rise and slope, whether it installed at grade or above grade (the preference is slightly above grade for drainage if the building code allows it), and whether it is straight, winding, or has sharp turns. There might even need to be one or more flat intermediate landings.

Also, the landscaping and other obstacles along the walkway is an important safety consideration to keep in mind with the possibility of someone veering from the hard surface or debris encroaching on the surface.

By creating a design feature with your entry walk, you will have differentiated yourself in the market and given your homeowners convenience, safety, accessibility, visitability, and more value as a result.

# 7

# Universal Design Means Greater Appeal

## Universal Design Is Differentiating

Since universal design as a concept is not commonly employed into new construction, you will be making a positive statement about the quality and value of your homes without ever using either of those two terms.

Every builder wants to be known as someone who builds quality and delivers value.

In fact, many builders use one or both words in the name of their company or in their tagline.

It has gotten so common that the impact of both words has become diluted and diminished.

However, saying or expressing that you build quality or that you create or provide value by using other words, phrases, concepts, actions, or construction details can have an even greater impact.

People will readily tell that you offer quality and value by what they see — and the way you describe what you have done and why it is beneficial for the consumer.

When you pay attention to subtle details and convey to the customer that you have designed your homes to take into account their safety, peace-of-mind, enjoyment, comfort, convenience, accessibility, return-on-investment, and ability for their friends and family to visit them easily, you have demonstrated more about your concern for quality and value than a slogan ever could.

Universal design as I have shown you in this text does just that.

## Universal Design Is Memorable

One of the keys to effectively selling new homes is to create one or more memory points for your customers to latch onto and take with them.

You want them to remember you distinctly — and in a very positive way — from the other builders they have seen or considered.

While universal design is supposed to fit seamlessly into the overall layout and construction of the home so that what you have done is not obvious — unless you have an educated consumer that is specifically looking for such items — there is certainly no reason for you and your sales team to let it remain unobtrusive and invisible.

You need to point out what you have done, why you decided to it, and what it means to them.

This helps to anchor your design elements in their minds and become the memory points that want them to remember and take away about you and your homes above all the others in the marketplace.

You don't need signs or anything showy to point out what you've done.

Just describe and illustrate the features with an emotional benefit statement for each one.

Your customers will get the message and will even help share what you are doing with their friends.

## Universal Design And Your Sales Program

Even when people aren't familiar with universal design or aren't specifically looking for it, they will appreciate having it included in your homes when you explain why you have used it and what it means to them.

First, they will be getting more included features than anyone else in your price point offers — regardless of what your price point or home sizes happen to be.

Second, you will have devoted much more attention to your homeowners' safety, accessibility, personal comfort, convenience, and enjoyment of their living space that any other builder in your marketplace.

Third, their homes will be designed to be accessible by nearly anyone — members of their household, extended family, guests, or visitors — without any special accommodations or adaptations.

Fourth, they won't need to hire remodelers or anyone else after they move in to make universal design modifications since you will already have done that — even if you charge a little more for your homes to cover it.

Fifth, they will find that the home will allow them to remain living comfortably in it for as long as they like because of the design elements and strategies you have included.

Sixth, they will have the potential for higher value retention, greater resale value, broader consumer acceptance, and a faster future sale because of the many features you have included in the home that result in widespread market appeal.

It doesn't matter how you help your customers shop for their new home — as a small volume or custom home builder that sells your own homes and interfaces directly with your customers, or as a builder that employs a professional sales staff (or brokers) of one or more people to conduct your sales presentations.

These concepts will translate into more sales as you engage your customers and explain the tremendous value and benefits in the design choices you have made and have available for them.

## Utilizing A Team Approach

For many of the universal design concepts, strategies, and solutions presented in this text, you will want to involve other professionals to work with you who can help you implement these changes and solutions.

This means relying more than normal on your typical trades to advise you and take an active role in creating the strategies, solutions, and concepts you are seeking.

It also means seeking the professional input of consultants such as architects, occupational therapists, kitchen and bath designers, interior designers, and durable medical equipment suppliers.

In addition, your marketing materials — websites, collateral pieces, direct mail, print and electronic ads, blogs, and social sites — need to convey to the public that you build your homes with a universal design emphasis to attract a larger following for your homes.

Get your model merchandisers or stagers to help also in conveying your message to your customers.

## Now, It's Up To You

The universal design concepts, treatments, solutions, tips, recommendations, and strategies that I present in this book are for you use in designing, marketing, building, and selling your new homes — and to give you a competitive edge in your marketplace.

Use them to increase the selection of homes that offer accessibility, safety, comfort, and convenience.

You may already be using some of these design elements. That's a great start, and now you can add to what's already been done.

I have given you many ways to really distinguish yourself in your marketplace and provide a valuable service to your customers.

Now, it's up to you to begin incorporating these features into your designs. As you move forward, I'm available as a resource for you.

# Steve Hoffacker

**Steve Hoffacker**, CAPS, C.E.A.C., STEVE HOFFACKER LLC, based in West Palm Beach, Florida, is a Certified Aging-In-Place Specialist (CAPS), a Certified Environmental Access Consultant (C.E.A.C.), a consistent writer and blogger on aging-in-place topics, an approved Instructor for the National Association of Home Builder's (NAHB) University of Housing aging-in-place, universal design, and remodeling sales and marketing courses, and an approved provider of continuing education courses for the National Kitchen & Bath Association (NKBA).

Steve was honored as the 2015 "CAPS Educator of the Year" by the NAHB and has graduated well over 500 professionals through the CAPS designation program.

For more than 30 years as a new construction consultant and more than 10 years as a CAPS Instructor, he has helped homebuilders, contractors and remodelers, interior designers, kitchen and bath designers, architects, occupational therapists, physical therapists, DME providers, nurses, physicians, university faculty, non-profit organizations, governmental agencies, building materials manufacturers and showrooms, and many others to be more visible, competitive, profitable, and effective – and to really enjoy themselves as they pursue their business and create wonderful customer experiences and solutions that allow people to remain living in their chosen homes.

www.stevehoffacker.com
www.aginginplaceinsider.com

www.ingramcontent.com/pod-product-compliance
Lightning Source LLC
Chambersburg PA
CBHW070919180426
43192CB00038B/1870